THE CITY GRUMP RIDES OUT

THE CITY GRUMP
RIDES OUT

The City Grump

Matador
9 Priory Business Park,
Wistow Road, Kibworth Beauchamp,
Leicestershire. LE8 0RX
Tel: 0116 279 2299
Email: books@troubador.co.uk
Web: www.troubador.co.uk/matador
Twitter: @matadorbooks

ISBN 978 1789017 809

British Library Cataloguing in Publication Data.
A catalogue record for this book is available from the British Library.

Printed and bound by CPI Group (UK) Ltd, Croydon, CR0 4YY
Typeset in 11pt Adobe Caslon Pro by Troubador Publishing Ltd, Leicester, UK

Matador is an imprint of Troubador Publishing Ltd

To natural grumps everywhere

TABLE OF CONTENTS

INTRODUCTION

"Power is the best shield that the disordered personality
can conceive against being revealed as the laughing stock
he secretly suspects himself to be."

William Donaldson

"The Letters of Henry Root" written by William Donaldson left a lasting impression on me. They must have done because I read them shortly after they were published in book form, way back in 1980. Henry Root was the nom de plume of Donaldson who took great delight in writing to the great, the good, and the otherwise. His aim, through the unleashing of very politically incorrect suggestions in his letters, was to use this satirical prose to throw a revealing spotlight onto his targets.

In a way the City Grump blogs in the online magazine, Real Business, are my attempt to emulate the pomposity-pricking element of the unsurpassable Henry Root. Of course in the days of my full time employment in the City, it would have been impossible to publish such pieces, but once free of such commitment from early 2010 and onward I had and have no such inhibitions. Bliss!

The idea of the City Grumps is to root (sic) out some of the absurdities perpetrated by our leaders and institutions on us poor citizenry. I guess one advantage of having worked in the City for more than a quarter of a century is I was able to observe many of the powerful at close range. What I discovered, however gradually, was that indeed "Power is the best shield that the disordered personality can conceive against being revealed as the laughing stock he secretly suspects himself to be." Investigative journalists have always known this and, before the national newspapers found themselves losing both circulation and influence we could rely on enough of them being around to shine a much needed light on such people and institutions. Now there is Private Eye and not much more.

The City Grump is my little homage to that fantastic scene in the film Network (recently restaged at the National Theatre) where the national newscaster Howard Beale (played by Peter Finch), railing at the dissemblance of the powerful, urges his viewers to get off their backsides, go to their windows and yell "I'm as mad as hell and I am not going to take this anymore". The difference is that I hope in many instances I have put forward practical solutions to some of the calumnies at hand.

This book is a compendium of what I like to think are the most apposite City Grumps. It is split into six different headings each with an introductory commentary. To use that invasive Americanism, "Enjoy"!

CHAPTER 1

THE GOOD, THE BAD AND THE HOPELESS

"Attitude is a little thing that makes a big difference."

Winston Churchill.

Much of this chapter is given over to City Grumps on powerful people, be they political and/or rich, together with groups of the influential and their attitudes. Reading these pieces again it certainly makes me wonder, given the fault lines examined here, why do so many seek power over the rest of us? Is it some subconscious yearning for the pre-war days when even many in the middle classes had servants to boss around? Or is it that it is just so intoxicating? I rather like the American author, Elizabeth Gilbert's take:

"I met an old lady once, almost a hundred years old, and she told me, 'There are only two questions that human beings have ever fought over, all through history. How much do you love me? And who's in charge?"

There is of course Margaret Thatcher's characteristically rapier-like observation that "being powerful is like being a lady. If you have to tell people you are, you aren't."

In the following you'll meet many familiar characters and institutions (Branson, Carney, Davos, Murdoch, Socialism, Thatcher) but there is also a sprinkling of the less well known, often brimming with admirable attitude. Truly a mix of the good, the bad and the hopeless.

1 October, 2010

Why do we admire the killer instinct?

On his brother's condemnation of the Iraq war, David Miliband turned to Harriet Harman and said: "You voted for it, why are you clapping?" Harman replied: "I'm clapping because, as you know, I'm supporting him." This exchange says everything you need to know about the re-emergence of Stalinist type leadership.

The descriptions of Ed Miliband's victory over his brother to become boss of the Labour party have led commentators to conclude that, well of course, Ed has that much needed "killer instinct" that David lacks.

Possession of the killer instinct increasingly seems to be regarded as a desirable and admirable asset in the boardroom these days. If you don't play up to that attribute, how are you going to have the drive needed to propel the company onwards and upwards? How are you going to close those all-important deals? I wouldn't mind betting that Lord Browne's colleagues at BP believed he had the killer instinct and the same probably goes for Dick Fuld at Lehman's as well as a host of other high-profile business figures. The fact that Browne and Fuld's business careers ended in tears doesn't seem to dissuade many of us from being drawn ineluctably towards those with the killer instinct. Ask Harriet Harman – or those close to Stalin and Hitler for that matter.

My instinct tells me that if you want to lay the foundations for a long and successful business, you're better off identifying intelligent, knowledgeable employees who are more interested in finding ways to grow the business than fighting their way to the top by hook or by crook. If you reward those employees with praise, position and cash, then you are on the road to creating a broad-based and profitable enterprise.

Alternatively you could follow Ed Miliband's example and countless people before him: identify a fundamentally weak and unstable organisation, single-mindedly cut a swathe through all obstacles in your path and emerge all smiley-faced at the top of the pile.

But can you live with all those bad odours that you set loose on the way?

26 October, 2010

Are baby boomers inherently selfish?

A recent fascinating lecture, a letter to a national newspaper and Lord Browne's recommendations on student fees make me wonder whether my generation of baby boomers has become irredeemably selfish.

The lecture was given by William Hopper, co-author of a wonderful book called the Puritan Gift and, at 83, most definitely not a baby boomer. He pointed out that when he became a director of Morgan Grenfell in the early seventies, he was paid twice the amount of his secretary. In those days, Morgan Grenfell was regarded as a top notch merchant bank. How, he asked, could someone in the equivalent post today deserve a multiple of 100 times that?

The letter was from Bill Whiting, written to the Daily Telegraph shortly after Lord Browne's proposals on university fees were published. It read:

"Young people faced with repaying their tuition costs, while struggling to save to buy a home and funding an older generation's burgeoning pension and health costs, may well become more than miffed with the deal – and even more so as they hear squeals of protest at any hint of means-testing of free bus passes, winter fuel allowances and television licences. To top it all, there are some of us baby boomers who would like to leave the epic national debt for our children to pay, too, rather than take the pain of tackling it ourselves. There was a time, we may recall, when we would have taken to the streets to protest against far less significant grievances."

Wherever you look in big corporations and public institutions, at national and local level, there are countless examples of employees awarded salaries that their fathers' generation would have regarded as ridiculous. Yet these same people blithely say to the next generation: "If you want to go to university, then you must pay and pay handsomely." There is much sanctimonious twittering about how universities are just another marketplace and therefore students must pay a market rate. By that logic, why not get all students in higher education over the age of 16 to pay for their A-level courses as well?

The sad fact is that my generation has had it all. Free education, over-inflated salaries, a "spend, spend, spend" mentality and, apart from occasional terrorist activity, peace on the home front. Education is the bedrock of a civilised society. To tell our children to cough up is yet another abrogation of responsibility by us baby boomers. We, meaning the State, individuals and companies, owe it to them to dig deep.

19 July, 2011

News Corp: a culture run amuck

Everyone blames "rampant nepotism and failed corporate governance" for the News Corp scandal. But a bunch of non-execs and a pile of corporate governance manuals wouldn't have made a blind bit of difference.

I remember meeting Rupert Murdoch in the very early nineties when he was doing the rounds of the City looking for money to alleviate his then highly indebted empire. It was like having a caged leopard in the room.

The idea that he had to be there to give an account of himself to others made him spit and snarl. We concluded that indeed he was a brilliant entrepreneur but we would stand no chance, as non- family investors, of ever having any hold on him if things started to go wrong.

Herein lies the myth of corporate governance. In cases such as News Corp, up goes the cry of: "If only there had been good corporate governance then the News of the World fiasco would never have happened". This is nonsense.

The way an entity conducts itself is down to its state of mind and that comes straight from the top. When employees at the News of the World hacked into thousands of citizens' phones, they were carrying on a long tradition that stretches back to the murder of Thomas a Becket by four Knights who thought they were doing the King's bidding. As with Becket's assassins, I would argue that a culture of "the end justifies the means" has grown up in the Murdoch organisation.

You can't teach integrity, either the leader has it or they don't. No amount of stuffing boards with the so-called great and the good, or waving corporate governance manuals about, is going to change the spots on the leopard.

The Murdoch odyssey can provide a useful lesson for all of us weighing up whether to invest in company X or do business with company Y. Is the company in question operated by a driven individual (hopefully yes) and, if so, is it run with integrity?

Remember: words are not enough. Here are some from News Corp's Mission Statement:

"We never give or take kickbacks or bribes"

"We take our corporate social responsibilities seriously"

"We are committed to fostering a high-trust work environment for our employees".

Well, at least it made me laugh….

5 August, 2011

Corporate jargon: "What I really meant to say was…"

As times get harder, have you noticed how our movers and shakers come up with ever more deceptive phrases to gloss over difficult situations?

Politicians are, naturally, absolute masters of the art. So: "Let me be absolutely clear on this point" translates as: "I'm now going to take you as far away from this issue as I possibly can."

Another gem is: "Of course there is a lot more work to be done" meaning: "We have no idea at all how to deal with this problem."

I came across one government minister who said in print recently: "I am pushing through radical reform to make sure that the mistakes of the past are not repeated." Has he stopped to think that turning everything upside down will probably result in a whole new series of mistakes? This kind of muddle-headedness has caused endless chaos in our health and education systems for generations.

Another rich source of smoke and mirrors can often be found in the chairman's statement accompanying the company's accounts. These usually start with the splendid phrase: "It gives me great pleasure to present" when they really should say: "Oh God, it's that time of year again."

In the current economic torpor, the words: "Conditions remain challenging" can be found all over the place, whereas: "We are just about hanging on in there" would be nearer the truth.

Just in case such phraseology makes you want to reach for the glass of whisky and the loaded revolver, many chairmen then resort to the time-honoured: "We are leveraging our core competencies" which I think means: "We are trying to get back to what we are actually supposed to be good at." Ah, so there is hope? Not when he or she rounds off the statement with the well-worn: "We are well-placed to take advantage of the upturn", which means: " If things don't improve soon, we'll be a gonner before my next chairman's statement is due."

Mind you, in its interim results this week, Barclays surpassed all of the above by announcing: "We are focused on creating happy customers and positive operating jaws." Wow, steady on tiger!

Meanwhile back in the boardroom, there is a whole variety of weasel words at play, such as: "We need more granularity on this". In my view anyone who comes up with this twaddle should be fired on the spot. The dictionary tells me that granularity is the breaking down of tasks into smaller and more manageable parts. Well, why not say so then?

To help you out with a few further translations:

"Joe Bloggs has done the heavy lifting on this one" means "Joe Bloggs has actually done what he is paid to do."

"We need to improve the optics" means "It would be nice to be more transparent but, in reality, we need to cover our tracks."

"Can we take this offline?" means "I know I'm going to lose this argument we are having and I don't want to look like a complete chump in front of the whole board."

It seems only fitting I should round off with a line that media master Rupert Murdoch recently fed to the House of Commons Select Committee...

"This is the most humble day of my life" means "Dammit, I'm not as good as I thought I was."

1 February, 2012

The beginning of the end for monster pay packets?

There's an interesting letter from a Mr Ian Cameron (any relation to Dave?) in this week's Telegraph. Here, Cameron points out when he was a banker, no bonuses were written into their contracts of employment and that "at no time should individuals, departments or divisions be awarded bonus payments when the holding or group company does not make a profit".

Is this laughably unrealistic today and in the future?

Not according to an article by Gillian Tett in the Financial Times, which highlights research into Wall Street pay over the past 150 years.

For much of this period, financial-sector pay relative to the rest of the private sector was roughly at parity. This changed to 1.7 times in the run-up to the crash of 1929 and again it hit 1.7 in 2006, just as sub- prime mania was climaxing.

But in a world of technological change and globalisation, you need bright highly skilled bankers right? Wrong. In a splendid de-bunking of this nonsense, the researchers point out "the technological development of the past 40 years (with IT in particular) should have disproportionately increased efficiency", noting that in companies such as Walmart, efficiency has reduced wages.

The researchers calculate that at least half the relative pay jump in the financial sector represents skimming off fees, not innovation.

Tett goes on to argue that recent changes in the remuneration models at the likes of Goldman Sachs, Morgan Stanley and JP Morgan Chase are the first signs that pay could be on a slow-but-sure journey back to historic parity.

I think she is right. There are obviously the high-profile political casualties such as Hester and Goodwin but at the more workaday level, financial companies and their stakeholders are beginning to realise that there is an almost endless supply of bright young graduates who would be only too pleased to learn how to step into the shoes of those who complain they can't get by on £200k a year.

Global financial institutions keep their wheels turning by making sure their employees conform to strict routines. They are "worker bees", not successful financial entrepreneurs. Hence maintaining pay scales at anywhere near 1.7 times the private sector average is, quite simply, unsustainable. Not that the boards of RBS (staff bonus pool of £500m) and Barclays (staff bonus pool last year of £2.7bn) have twigged this yet.

No doubt Simon Walker, director-general of the Institute of Directors, would describe my article as yet another example of "anti-business hysteria". Deep down he probably knows that many of his FTSE 100 directors also cannot hope to carry on being paid well over the odds for just being "upstairs employees" of their regular-as-clockwork companies.

Modern capitalism needs to be about high rewards for successful entrepreneurs. Those who can do nothing better with their lives than attach themselves to Megacorp will find that the days of megabucks are drawing to a close. And not before time.

9 April, 2013

The right and honourable Margaret Thatcher

I was incredibly fortunate to start my financial career in 1979 when Margaret Thatcher came to power. In my previous 25 years I had watched my country undergo a slow motion car crash. That ended with her.

In just about everything she did she was right and she was honourable and don't let the feeble minded of today convince you otherwise.

For many who were not starting out in the 1970s it is probably very hard to imagine what a hopeless country we had become. The term "private enterprise" didn't really exist. The world of work was dominated by union power. If a business wanted a new telephone line put in the only way to get it done in under three months was to bribe a GPO employee. Property owning was for the few. Britain was the sick man of Europe. The Superpowers, America and the USSR regarded us with disdain.

All that changed in the eleven years she was prime minister. It is entirely down to her and her determined chancellors that there is an SME sector today, that entrepreneurs are able to get their enterprises off the ground and that people want to do business with Britain.

She was right to destroy union power, right to open up the financial system and right to keep the stifling bureaucracy of Brussels and the recidivists of Strasbourg at bay.

She was deeply honourable. She was not for turning. Her principles were clear. She never wavered from her belief that it was the individual who should have the right to choose his/her destiny and that the State most definitely does not know best.

Eventually, of course her implacable resolve was to prove too much for our political establishment which is schooled in blowing with the wind. Her timid colleagues saw their chance to remove her when her Poll Tax policy stirred up riots in central London and elsewhere. Out she went and more fool the Conservative Party. They have not really recovered since. The slick and weasel worded Tony Blair stole most of her political clothes but never had her integrity and grit. No one would describe him as "The Iron Man". The current Westminster generation are but Lilliputians.

Rest in peace, Margaret, and thank God you are no longer here to witness the developing omnishambles at home and abroad.

9 July, 2013

Knowledge is power and power corrupts

Knowledge is power and power corrupts. It's time we understood the full implications of Edward Snowden's revelations for finance and commerce as well as for the man on The Clapham Omnibus.

I find it really extraordinary that after the initial interest in Snowden's unmasking of the near limitless data mining that goes on by government sponsored surveillance, most of the press and the public – both here and in the US – has relapsed into the lackadaisical response, "Well what do you expect in this age of terrorism and social media?"

Germany, France, Spain and Italy, all of whom can still remember the horrors of State surveillance under fascist regimes seem, after widespread indignation, to have retreated back to their comfy offices and restaurants. The implication of such attitudes is that Snowden is nothing more than a common traitor to his country.

Every now and again someone tries to re awaken the public's brains such as Stephen Walt, Harvard professor of international affairs, writing in this week's Financial Times, suggesting provocatively that Snowden deserves an immediate presidential pardon.

He remarks that "history will probably be kinder to Mr Snowden than to his pursuers, and his name may one day be linked to other brave men and women – Daniel Ellsberg, Martin Luther King, Mark Felt, Karen Silkwood and so on – whose acts of principled defiance are now widely admired".

Walt observes that "under the veneer of 'national security', government officials can use these vast troves of data to go after anyone, questioning what they were doing, including whistleblowers investigative journalists or ordinary citizens posting comments on news websites. Once a secret surveillance system exists, it is only a matter of time before someone abuses it for selfish ends".

And here's the rub. Edward Snowden was a young contractor who decided to go public on abuses as he saw it, yet there are hundreds of other unseen men and woman working away at GCHQ, and its US equivalent, with access to a treasure trove of private information.

At their fingertips is a wealth of information on upcoming stock market deals, company takeovers, company IP, drug formulae, nascent political decisions, meeting schedules and so on. The possibilities for those on the surveillance inside track to make money from using such information are infinite.

For example, I will bet a pound to a pinch of salt that the source of a number of insider driven stock price movements can be traced back to someone glued to a computer screen at GCHQ/NSA. It is naïve beyond belief to think that no one in there is using this "legitimised" information for their own personal financial gain. Yet I have not seen any discussion of this unintended consequence of the so-called fight against terrorism.

So next time you are taken aback that someone seems to have cottoned on to that conversation you were having about taking over your principle competitor or launching a game changing product, you might like to tell those charged with enforcing the law, be it the FCA or the police, where they should direct some of their enquiries.

As Country Life, my next favourite publication after Real Business, puts it, "Universal surveillance can't be justified in a free society. If we continue to allow it, the terrorists will have won and our enlightened, liberal society will be no more."

Corruption will rule the roost.

27 September 2013

The cancer of Socialism is out of remission. Why?

Tony Blair and his team of specialists administered some powerful New Labour drugs on the patient but now he is out of remission. How so?

Milliband Jnr has dominated the headlines this week with his cry of "we'll stop your snowballing energy bills". The fact that this crackpot price control policy wasn't immediately laughed out of the land tells you that there is something far deeper at issue here. Here's why:

Socialism spreads when it is able to feed off highly visible blatant abuses of financial privilege and right now conditions for its destructive ingress are near perfect. Why? Because there is an intolerable mismatch of the rewards paid to managers at the top of their particular trees and those struggling to cling to the branches.

KPMG's 2012 survey of FTSE 100 Directors' BASIC salaries found that the average CEO was given over £800k and other Executive Directors approximately £500k last year. FTSE 250 equivalents were a mere £450k and £300k respectively. In all 350 companies, KPMG recorded that when you add in bonuses, share incentive schemes, etc, these ladies and gentleman trebled their remuneration.

These directors, together with massively high packages for those at the top of NHS, Local Authority and numerous other trees, are what the press and the politicians refer to as "Fat Cats". This is insulting to cats as they are naturally resourceful and independent minded creatures. Apart from a miniscule number of exceptions, such as Sorrell at WPP, these people have never had to take the risk of building a business or financing an entrepreneur. Instead, they have carefully climbed the corporate ladder and stepped into the pre-determined world of the company board room.

Once in place they have been content to spend cash on themselves rather than on developing their companies. The FT reported last week that FTSE 100 companies are sitting on their largest cash piles ever recorded – a classic example of timidity rather than grasping opportunities thrown up by recessionary times.

I would prefer to call them Sloths. Google tells me that "after consuming a large meal two-thirds of the Sloth's bodyweight will consist of the contents of its stomach". Contrast then, these enormous feasts with the diet that the rest of us have been asked to go on for the last five years following previous excess, then it is plain as a pikestaff why Socialists are going to get a hearing between now and the next election.

Is there anything that can be done to combat this situation? Some would say tax the Sloths more heavily but that is a Socialist doctrine. The institutional investors in these companies should demand large cuts in their packages and ignore egregious nonsense about "we will lose all our best people" – there will be no shortage of younger talented staff willing to take main board directorships for half the current going rate.

29 January, 2014

The failure of the Davos elite

I am not a natural fan of Martin Wolf, one of the FT's senior commentators, but earlier this month he produced an absolute corker of an article on the world's elites. I am indebted, for much of the following, to him.

Wolf argues that "complex societies rely on their elites to get things, if not right, at least not grotesquely wrong. When elites fail, the political order is likely to collapse....The dire results of elite failures are not surprising.

"An implicit deal exists between elites and the people: the former obtain the privileges and perquisites of power and property; the latter, in return, obtain security and, in modern times, a measure of prosperity. If elites fail, they risk being replaced."

Last week a great swathe of the economic, bureaucratic and intellectual elites (together with a smattering of the usual smug media stars) gathered for their annual Davos love-in.

Should we look up to and respect these men and women? Of course not. Most of them are abject failures. Wolf pinpoints three areas where they have failed, and they pretty much cover the waterfront of our lives.

Wolf's first is: "the economic, financial, intellectual and political elites mostly misunderstood the consequences of headlong financial liberalisation. Lulled by fantasies of self-stabilising financial markets, they not only permitted but encouraged a huge and, for the financial sector, profitable bet on the expansion of debt.

"The policy making elite failed to appreciate the incentives at work and, above all, the risks of a systemic breakdown.... economies collapsed; unemployment jumped; and public debt exploded. The policy making elite was discredited by its failure to prevent disaster. The financial elite was discredited by needing to be rescued.

"The political elite was discredited by willingness to finance the rescue. The intellectual elite-the economists- was discredited by its failure to anticipate a crises or agree on what to do after it had struck.

"The rescue was necessary. But the belief that the powerful sacrificed taxpayers (and I might add savers) to the interest of the guilty is correct."

The second failure Wolf identifies is: "in the past three decades we have seen the emergence of a globalised economic and financial elite. Its members have become ever more detached from the countries that produced them. In the process, the glue that binds any democracy-the notion of citizenship- has weakened.

"The narrow distribution of the gains of economic growth greatly enhances this development. This, then, is ever more a plutocracy. A degree of plutocracy is inevitable in democracies built, as they must be, on market economies. But it is always a matter of degree.

"If the mass of the people view their economic elite as richly rewarded for mediocre performance and interested only in themselves, yet expecting rescue when things go badly, the bonds snap. We may be just at the beginning of this long term decay".

And who do we see bestriding the stage at Davos? One Jamie Dimon, boss of JP Morgan, a bank that faced massive fine after fine after fine in 2013. Any sign of him resigning, being sent to jail? No. Instead he has just been given a 74 per cent pay increase taking him to $20m!

Then we have our very own Mark Carney who, on arrival last year, declared that from his time onwards the Bank of England would be providing valuable forward guidance on interest rates.

Seven months later, with unemployment moving swiftly down to his trigger point for interest rate increases, his policy has been blown to smithereens. At the time I suspected him of being principally a smooth talking showman and now we know.

Any sign of him saying sorry that his big idea was wrong? No. Instead he is on a platform at Davos grinning away with that other master (mistress?) of the smoke and mirrors, Christine Lagarde of the IMF. Amazingly some of our citizenry still seem prepared to give him the benefit of the doubt. Not for much longer methinks.

Finally Wolf comes to the Euro where "the Europeans took their project beyond the practical into something far more important to people: the fate of their money. Nothing was more likely than frictions among Europeans over how their money was being managed or mismanaged...Yet it is the constitutional disorder of the Eurozone that is least emphasised.

"Within the Eurozone, power is now concentrated in the hands of the governments of the creditor countries, principally Germany, and a trio of unelected bureaucracies – the European Commission, the European Central Bank, and the International Monetary Fund.

"The peoples of adversely affected countries have no influence upon them. The politicians who are accountable to them are powerless. This divorce between accountability and power strikes at the heart of any notion of democratic governance".

And who pops up at Davos? None other than the ineffably smooth, though unelected, Sir Martin Sorrell of mega advertising corporation WPP, urging David Cameron to drop a referendum on Europe as he would then be "a shoo-in" for the next General Election. What bubble is he living in?

Meanwhile, back in London we have our own home grown elite in the House of Lords, talking out the Referendum Bill. If you look carefully you'll see that many of those Lordships are Davos aficionados as well.

Too many of those who frequent Davos are the elite with the same old faces and organisations. As Martin Wolf suggests, the implicit deal between Davosians and the citizenry has failed. They would be well advised to abandon their annual love fest in a fortified Swiss resort, go home, and spend the rest of this decade re-engaging with the other 99.9 per cent of the world. If they don't, there will be big trouble ahead.

14 April 2014

My business idea: Rude restaurants

Is it me or has the false bonhomie pendulum swung too far? I have just the business proposal to take advantage of the coming backlash.

Have you noticed these days how in every shop chain or high street bank you visit, the end of the transaction is marked by the hapless assistant mouthing "enjoy the rest of your day" at you?

Clearly there is some devastatingly effective training establishment, no doubt operating out of a bland office block in Slough that has persuaded HR departments up and down the land to drill into their frontline staff that this kind of utterance is life enhancing.

Last week, just as I was finishing making my contribution to the P&L of the local Mercedes garage, the assistant took this robotic display one step beyond when he said to me "and what are your plans for the rest of the day?"

I was so stunned by this that I opened my mouth but nothing came out. I suppose I should have said something like "Well at 2pm I'm going to set fire to the cat. At 3pm I'm planning on fixing the leaking tap in the kitchen the Memsahib has been on about and at 4pm I shall be running naked down Tonbridge High St in protest at impending parking charge increases", and then sat back to watch his expression.

So I think the time has come for an entirely new kind of business. Let's start a chain of restaurants/gastropubs, which are the complete antithesis of such mind reducing false bonhomie.

For example staff would wear t-shirts with the slogan "Don't even think of complaining". Ideal front of house employees could be resting actors who would be encouraged to engage customers in badinage such as "surely that dress doesn't go with those shoes?" and "after slogging through that main course do you really need a pudding?", instead of "is everything alright for you?" (listen lady if it wasn't, you'd know by now).

Of course the food and drink would have to be top notch for the money, the speed of service impeccable, and the banter capable of being changed regularly.

Central London is where most new trends start so we should launch there. I'm pretty sure we'd soon be the talk of the town, trending on twitter (I think that's the expression) and well on the way to making our fortune.

So, dear reader, if you have leisure industry experience and ready to embark on a chain of non PC eateries then let me know. You might have a financial backer!

11 August 2014

Gatwick versus the people

Down here in the Garden of England, to paraphrase Peter Finch in one of the all-time movie greats, "Network", we are as mad as hell and we are not going to take it anymore.

What is inducing such rage against the system? Gatwick, that's what.

This has it all. Big business, owned by faceless foreigners, makes bid to persuade the Establishment that they have found the line of least resistance in achieving the massive increase in airplane movements that the current political mindset demands.

Step 1: issue, sotto voce, an incomprehensible Ipsos Mori Consultation (London Airspace Change. Local Area Consultation).

Step 2: experiment by sending aircraft down one superhighway corridor over the heads of country bumpkins who haven't the resources to fight back.

Step 3: ...ah yes well they hadn't counted on the likes of Steve Haysom and thousands of other individuals and local businesses upsetting the Gatwick applecart. Here are the highlights from his broadside to second Gatwick runway junkie, Paul Carter leader of Kent County Council.

After years of platitudes, across the spectrum, from our dissembling masters Haysom is as mad as hell and can you blame him? If you'd like to join him at a national level, then Howard Davies at airports.delivery@airports.gsi.gov.uk is waiting to hear from you, but no later than this Friday!

The creation of the proposed airborne 'Superhighway' will cause massive harm to great swathes of the county and the creation of a second runway will blight one of the most beautiful parts of the country in an act of wanton vandalism.

"That's the price of progress" cry supporters of the scheme and the alleged £50 billion benefit to the economy would come in handy if you believe for a single second that such a benefit would accrue or that any of those currently engaged in the "my scheme's bigger than your scheme" willy waving have the slightest idea what the upside might be.

It does not take a lot of effort to identify examples of where the Great British Public have been contemptuously fobbed off with a heady mixture of propaganda, crass incompetence and often downright lies – weapons of mass destruction? Err, no; tiny trickle of Eastern Europeans, no.

It can only be hoped that the recent rise of UKIP causes the political elite as well as hordes of bureaucrats to remember whom they exist to serve and start to treat their employers with a little more respect – "fancy a referendum on PR?" No, not really bothered, wouldn't mind one on Europe though, 'come on, you only had one on the Common Market in 1975'.

Ironically this predicted economic boon is very close to the cost of HS2 – another lemon the GBP would almost certainly reject given their say.

Red Ed would have to work long and hard to secure my vote next May, but even I can see that even if such spectacularly enhanced prosperity were to accrue, the current inequality in this country will result in very little, if any, trickling down to those afflicted – how about asking the question "would you be OK with a reduction in your quality of life in exchange for an increase in wealth for a few fat cats?". Don't be surprised if the question is met with less than universal approbation.

But let's not ever lose sight of the fact that this is all about money.

Even with the advent of behemoths such as the Airbus A380, modern planes can be far quieter than those in even the recent past; the reason for the increasing nuisance is purely the fact that the airlines are operating in a way that saves them fuel – despite all assurances to the contrary the planes are so low over Chiddingstone (14 miles from Gatwick) I swear I can see who went for the chicken and who plumped for the beef.

"But don't we need more flights to China and the other emerging nations to remain at the economic top table?"

Arguably, but new technology released at the CES show in Las Vegas gave a glimpse of virtual 3D meetings, and why would anyone clamour to travel with their little bags of liquids and receipt for the tablet confiscated because the battery was flat, unless they really had to.

These plans are not designed to fuel the UK as an economic powerhouse, the terminal buildings at Gatwick are not thronging with be-suited City gents, they are rammed with corpulent, tattooed Sharons and Darrens on their way to Shagaluf.

If you need further proof that money is the motivation behind Gatwick's quest for a second runway, the fact that it ran a whole series of advertisements in the national press this week making its case should remove any lingering doubt.

"We believe so passionately that Gatwick offers the best solution to the UK economy that we are spending a fortune advertising the fact" or "Choose us and we can ship thousands of extra stag parties to Prague and make an absolute mint" – you decide.

Global Infrastructure Fund – the very-much-for-profit vehicle that owns Gatwick is domiciled in New York so there won't be many tears shed over the destruction of Hever Castle as long as the fund hits its target of 15-20 per cent gross returns.

Key early investors were Credit Suisse, which heavily promotes the fund, and General Electric.

The fund purchased Gatwick in 2009 and is clearly looking to maximise its investment – these funds are notoriously difficult to unpick but rest assured that English Heritage and the CPRE are not investors.

Oregon Investment Council however is and so are a number of sovereign wealth funds, endowment and corporate and public pensions funds from Maine, Oregon and Washington.

I know that what we are facing is nothing compared to the poor souls on flight ME17 – but it has been confirmed that the reason it was overhead a war zone despite all the warnings was that it was the most direct and therefore cheapest route to fly – completely outrageous but a very stark representation of where priorities lie in these matters.

I have never seen a rolling chalk landscape, a lazy summer stream, a misty water meadow or gently rustling shaw that would be enhanced by a plane thundering over it belching its load of poisonous filth; no picnic at nearby Hever Castle, school play at Chiddingstone Castle or walk through the local bluebell woods would benefit from the deafening roar of a plane coming in too low rendering conversation impossible.

If I, and others like me, don't stand up for this area who will? If that makes me a NIMBY then that is a tab that I am entirely comfortable with.

I never want to have to tell my grandchildren that "it used to be really nice around here but unfortunately a bunch of self-serving pen pushers ruined it and I did nothing to try to stop them".

I suspect that any attempt to mitigate what is happening by explaining that the Global Infrastructure Fund or the Abu Dhabi Investment Authority, National Pension Scheme of Korea, California Public Employees Retirement Scheme and the Future Fund of Australia have, however, achieved impressive returns on their investment, is likely to cut little mustard

I'm not sure what has changed of late, but the increase in noise is tangible and any further escalation will do irreparable damage to an area of outstanding natural beauty.

My boys recently sat their A/S levels and each complained that their sleep had been interrupted by the planes and that they fear their performance had been impaired.

I am undeniably irked that I can no longer enjoy a peaceful evening in the garden with a glass of something refreshing, but that will be as nothing if I believe that my children's life chances have been in any way hurt by people who would probably struggle to find Chiddingstone on a map and are more interested in the nature of their own legacy rather than the destruction they wreak along the way.

I suspect that it is harder to ask 'why are we running' rather than to just go with the flow, but I for one will not sit idly by and witness the destruction of the environment for no proven benefit; I challenge you to have the courage to join me by

1. Retracting Kent County Council support for Gatwick expansion
2. Rejecting the plans for the 'Superhighway'
3. Actively opposing Gatwick expansion and
4. Clarifying this position with the Airports Commission as a matter of urgency

The only thing that appears to have come in lower than the planes is the laughably entitled 'consultation process' that was sneaked in under the radar in January and I urge you to reject its conclusions as I believe that it was fraudulently conducted.

Much is made of the environmental impact of Boris Island, and I am all for preserving whatever we can, but inconveniencing a few ducks seems a small price to pay when compared to the destruction you support of the county you are elected to safeguard.

9 October 2014

Always look on the bright side of life

What have two ladies in an acute ward of a Parisian teaching hospital in common with a speech given by a recently retired British army major at a village church in Kent? Let me explain.

The two ladies, one a friend of mine of some 40 years and a very high flier in the OECD, the other a Senegalese immigrant to France, had been hovering between life and death for some days and were now showing small signs of improvement. My friend, Caroline, slowly realising what had happened to her and what she has in front of her, was in a mixture of despair and depression. She had been cut down by an abdominal aneurysm in her prime. One minute she was a cornerstone of the OECD's policy on Euro country bailouts and the next she was fighting off the grim reaper.

Back in Kent, Major Richard Streatfeild MBE, now retired from the British Army but not so long ago fighting in Afghanistan, gave a speech last Saturday at the launch of an exhibition cataloguing each of the 50 men from our village of Penshurst who lost their lives in World War I. One of these was his cousin Edwin.

Richard read out a letter written by his great uncle after 50 hours (yes, 50) of continuous action at the Somme in 1916. It described in unbelievably graphic detail the killing of "the hun" by his comrades and vice versa. He was the only officer of his company to survive that day. Sometime later he was awarded the Military Cross. He was killed on the 7th of November 1918, 5 days before the end of the war. The audience in Penshurst Church was stunned.

Unlike most of us who can only imagine what it is like, Richard Streatfeild saw death and destruction at the closest of quarters in Afghanistan and he admirably put across the potent mix of feelings that welled up inside him. As he said, almost under his breath, "every day is remembrance day" for him.

Caroline has made such a miraculous (her doctors' words, not mine) recovery that she was able to make a speech recently to a group of her oldest friends gathered at her Cambridge alma mater. What does she put the start of the road back to health down to? Her fellow Senegalese patient, who, seeing Caroline's great distress, said "what do you have to be sad about? Here we are warm, safe, and being cared for by wonderful medical staff while out there are so many people with no shelter, no food, no help".

To Caroline, who had been used to living life at the highest levels of society, this came as an absolute revelation and from then on she became determined to make the best of everything. Recovery followed in extraordinarily short order. The lesson she demanded we take away from her experience was of course, that we would be crazy to make anything other than the best of the hand life has given us.

Richard Streatfeild's experience of life has led him to reason that the most telling way he can describe what a battlefield is like is to imagine the worst and the best day you have ever known, as those are the emotions that run through you in the heat of war.

Two totally different experiences from totally different worlds and yet the message that Major Streafeild wanted to leave with us was exactly the same as Caroline's. Every day make the best of things. We may curse double dealing witless politicians, ignorant regulators, teeth grinding bureaucracy, disappointing staff, and on and on, but what the Richards and Carolines have been through makes it clear. The gift that keeps on giving is to, as the Pythons had it, "always look on the bright side of life".

3 November 2014

Is it time for Richard Branson to step out of the public spotlight?

For more years than I care to remember I have stared in goggle-eyed amazement at just how Richard Branson has been held in such high esteem by so many for so long.

Whether it is the Establishment's tick in the box of a knighthood or, for example, that survey in 2012, which voted him Britain's greatest entrepreneur in the first 60 years of our Queen's reign, his deification continues. Could it be that his spell is finally about to be broken after his latest and highest profile disaster in the Mojave Desert?

If you subscribe to the view that a leopard doesn't change his spots then the fact that one of Branson's earliest business enterprises ended up with him being thrown into jail for defrauding Customs & Excise was a worrying signal. This was a scheme to avoid paying tax on Virgin's merchandise by pretending to export record albums while actually selling them in the UK. Luckily for him his mother posted bail and he ended up negotiating a successful settlement of some £700,000 to avoid prosecution.

Until perhaps the other day, that was the low point for Branson. His first big break was the signing of Mike Oldfield to his record label who went on to record the gold mine that Tubular Bells became.

Along the way Branson has understandably hired and fired many senior employees. Some probably thought they deserved better but one was very high profile and died in tragic circumstances. Trevor Abbott had been his finance director for ten years and in 1997, just over a year after leaving Virgin, he was found hanging from a tree. This was how the Daily Mail reported the inquest:

"Two weeks before Christmas last year, the 47-year-old father of five filmed an eight-minute suicide note using the family camcorder. Some time later he was found hanging from a tree in a woodland near the £1m Abbott home in rural Surrey. The contents of the video were to remain outside the public domain, the coroner later decided. It was clear that Abbott had fully intended to end his life.

Conservative in habit and appearance, meticulous of detail and a tough negotiator in business, Abbott had long been the necessary counterweight at Virgin to Branson's 'gut instinct' and jumper-clad photo-opportunism. Indeed, as group managing director, Abbott had effectively run the empire on a day-to-day basis since the late 80s. More than once his sagacity had steered Virgin from the financial abyss that was threatened, some argue, by Branson's idiosyncratic approach.

In 2000 Tom Bower's biography of Branson observed: "Critics and admirers alike agreed that the Virgin Empire owed an incalculable debt to a sadly desperate man. Even Branson had acknowledged Abbott's indispensability. The Keeper of the Secrets had secured a substantial stake in the offshore trusts.

But in the months before his death, Abbott had been unable to persuade Branson to buy his shares for cash. As Abbott's business ventures faltered, Branson continued to reject his pleas for money.

"Like so many that thrive in the company of a tycoon, Abbott had discovered he lacked five essential qualities to emulate his former employer: ruthless energy, egoism, skill, instinct and, above all, a compelling performance. Over previous months, he had also discovered his lack of leverage over Branson. Abbott might know secrets but he would fear embarrassment, so remained silent. To buccaneers, men without leverage are not entitled to loyalty".

In 2013 the combative Tom Bower came back with an updated biography. Being something of a petrolhead, I was fascinated by Bower's account of Branson's involvement with Formula 1. In the depths of the financial recession Branson had very astutely managed to sponsor the Brawn GP team who, in a story worthy of Hollywood, went on to win the World Championship. Unfortunately for Branson the costs of running a team for the next season reverted to norm. Brawn went off to Mercedes and Bernie Ecclestone, realising Branson's reluctance to fully finance his own team's 2010 year, saw weakness as the FI circus commenced battle in Bahrain. Bower again: "After forty minutes he (Ecclestone) saw Virgin's cars pull out. "A nickel-and-dime operation" Ecclestone jeered "…Shit or get off the pot" Ecclestone told Branson as they passed in the paddock.

But the real centre of interest for the media, in reviewing Bower's latest biography, was his account of Branson's efforts to get paying tourists into space. The exciting sounding Virgin Galactic was born and so far circa 700 individuals (including the likes of Brad Pitt and Justin Bieber) have put down $80m in seat deposits. Bower pointed out that nothing much had gone

THE CITY GRUMP RIDES OUT

according to plan, not least of all the horrific death of three engineers during rocket engine testing in 2007.

Last week the grim reaper claimed another victim as Galactic's SpaceShipTwo blew up on a test flight. The Sunday Telegraph reports that the vice-president in charge of propulsion, the vice-president in charge of safety, and the chief aerodynamics engineer- had all quit Virgin Galactic in the last few months. Carolynne Campbell, the lead expert on rocket propulsion at the International Association for the Advancement of Space Safety said "This explosion is not a surprise. None whatsoever, I am sorry to say. It is exactly what I was expecting. It was Russian roulette which test flight blew up".

Something tells me that if that 2012 survey of Britain's greatest entrepreneur was run again today Branson would not be coming in at number one. Surely the time has come for him to quit the public spotlight, confine himself to his island of Necker (being fond of a joke he could always rename it Brass Necker), thus leaving the young and impressionable to focus their attention on some new British "hero"?

19 January 2015

Are we becoming too scared to laugh at authority?

A business colleague, while clearing out his attic, came across the following cutting taken from the Financial Times of 17th January 2000 "A London based fund manager has reached some conclusions as to the relative worth of some nationalities. It's all worked out by dividing countries' market capitalisation by their population-and it seems to show one Swiss is worth 3,761 Nigerians, a single American is worth 2 jumbo jets filled with Kenyans or Pakistanis (nb written pre 9/11) while one Israeli is worth 45 Iranians". We looked at each other and our first reaction was to wince and say wow, I bet the FT wouldn't dare publish that today. Probably not, but why not? Our politically correct antennae would twitch nervously but actually the research is intentionally funny and a great way of getting the reader to open his eyes. The author, Blakeney Asset Management is a well- respected investor in Africa and its message is that the low valuations of those emerging markets mean these countries have plenty of potential.

The power to laugh at religion took a horrific, brutal, knock in Paris. The persistence of some of the remaining cartoonists left alive there has led to a fearful mobilisation of armed police guards on the streets of cities all over the world. Thirty five years ago there was outrage amongst many Christians when Monty Python's Life of Brian satire on a child born in Nazareth being mistaken for the Messiah was released. Actually the power of its laughter delivered some very serious and effective messages, as one reviewer pointed out:

"This movie abounds with the longest list of priceless scenes in cinema history -- opening with a Sermon on the Mount for the aurally dyslexic and ending with a petty debate about whom gets crucified next to whom -- in which political correctness, resistance to progress, terrorist cell infighting, religious schism, social snobbery, feminism, chauvinism, imperialism, provincialism all take hard punches to the nose."

Indeed, the Reverend Professor Richard Burridge, who a year ago Pope Francis presented with the Vatican's top theological award, the first non-Roman Catholic to receive it, praised the film saying "What they did was take ordinary British people and transpose them into an historical setting and did a great satire on closed minds and people who follow blindly".

Britain's one full time female Muslim comedian, Shazia Mirza, writing in last week's Financial Times said "My faith is indestructible. I question it, laugh at it, even doubt it. It's important to ridicule things in order to understand them and that's why it is important to satirise Islam...if you can do that and allow others to laugh along, people will warm to you. They will learn about you instead of seeing you as outsiders they don't know much about. They will accept you, and you will prosper more easily".

Yes, and why shouldn't there be satire in the workplace as well? For example, I rather think that most highly paid FTSE 100 executives, together with their brethren gathering in Davos this week, continue to use a stultifying mixture of fear and political correctness to govern their employees. Actually they could learn a lot from the event that took place when I was incarcerated at a very austere house of learning in the 1960s-The Repton School Pedants. This was a pantomime performed by all members of staff that sent each other up and satirised some of the more notable school goings on of the time. It acted as a wonderful diffuser of tension (Paris was then in the news for the 1968 student riots and Lindsay Anderson had just released his seminal film "If") and helped bond teacher and pupil. The Pedants are still going strong to this day.

Demonstrating an ability to laugh at their own foibles and mistakes and encouraging their workforce to make fun of such could just produce the positive results that Burridge and Mirza, and even Repton School, highlight. Step forward "Drastic Dave" Lewis at Tesco.

12 July 2016

Is Mark Carney the most dangerous man in Britain?

Mark Carney needs no introduction – it seems wherever there is a podium, camera, or journalist there he is. So it comes as no surprise that the lure of the referendum and its result has proven irresistible to his natural tendency to speak out.

Central bankers know very well they are easy hostages to fortune so the wiser amongst their number adopt as low a public profile as possible. You would have thought Carney learnt this lesson when early on in his tenure he declared interest rates would rise if unemployment fell to seven per cent. As Sir John Scarlett was to Tony Blair in the run up to the Iraq war, Mark Carney supplied his prime minister with what he wanted to hear during the referendum campaign.

Accordingly he wasted no opportunity to issue dire warnings of what would become of the UK should we vote leave. He must have known this was a dangerously high profile, as in many quarters what the Governor of the Bank of England says still carries real weight.

When Mervyn King occupied that seat of power he would have confined himself to suitably delphic comments. Carney on the other hand is happy to set hares running in all kinds of direction. But it is in the post Brexit world that Carney is now well on the way to becoming the most dangerous man in Britain. First up was his half page interview with what sadly appears to have become a sort of rest home for bewildered "Remainers", the Financial Times. The interview highlighted one specific quote: "We are not going from a Rolls Royce to a Trabant overnight".

Well it's good to know we are okay for a day or two but not, according to Mr Carney, much longer. He might as well have added "eat drink and be merry for tomorrow we die". This kind of approach from our central banker is ludicrously irresponsible and downright dangerous. Not that he had finished there. Up he pops again in response to various property funds, post Brexit, closing their doors to redeemers of units.

Old faithful FT reported on Tuesday 5 July that "Britain's challenger banks have relatively high exposure to riskier lending, rendering them more exposed to an economic downturn than their larger established rivals. They also have a relatively high proportion of riskier commercial property loans on their books according to the BoE, which said that the commercial property market could be one of the key areas affected if overseas investors withdraw their money". The FT went on to note that shares in the challengers had dropped between ten and 15 per cent by early afternoon on Tuesday.

It's as well so few depositors read the FT, otherwise Carney might have caused a run on these new banks. He may have had a point, we don't know, but what I do know is that to go public with his doubts about these banks' viability is highly irresponsible and dangerous.

Quite apart from his foolish public utterances I also believe he is dangerously mismanaging interest rates.

In part Sterling remains weak because his Pavlovian response to hysterical wrong-footed Remain economists, together with possibility of falling property prices, is to drive interest rates to near zero. Yet again this may protect the British obsession with property but even a first year business student knows by now this does nothing for the productive economy, keeps Sterling in the sin bin, and encourages the taking on of evermore unproductive debt. Brilliant!

We can only hope that one of the first actions taken by Theresa May is to sack this most dangerous of men in Britain today.

12 January 2017

Davos leadership. Is there a pill for verbal indigestion?

In the run up to this year's Davos gathering of the great and the something or other, the founder of the World Economic Forum, Professor Klaus Schwab, issued an extraordinary one pager in the 11 January edition of the Financial Times.

Entitled "A Call for Responsive and Responsible Leadership", be prepared, dear reader, for what a friend of mine describes as "Naive Davosian Blairite tosh". Let me take you on a journey through this Davos leader's verbal fog.

It starts with: "It is the daunting task of today's leaders to take the right decisions in a complex world that suffers from many legacy issues and emotional turmoil. There cannot just be a return to basics! There has to be a recognition that we are in unmapped territory, which places the status quo, and by extension leaders themselves, into question. To fulfil this task, leaders need sensitivity and empathy to serve as their radar system and values and vision as their compass."

The sheer number of clichés in this paragraph would make any Hollywood film trailer voiceover immensely proud. How did "there cannot just be a return to basics!" get in there? Has Schwab just come from tea with Sir John and Lady Major? Did you know that today's radar systems can cater for sensitivity and empathy and you can buy a compass that points to values and vision

Schwab meanders on until he brings the reader up short with "we must invest substantially more into our physical, digital and social infrastructure, enabling current and future generations to have a purposeful life". Ah I see, so the mental and moral guidance evolved over 2000 years plus of mainstream religious thought can go hang so long as Davos man provides our kids with wi-fi enabled roofs over their heads and social services. That is the meaning of life.

"Leaders must be determined to ensure greater inclusiveness in the functioning of markets". Xavier Rolet, the SEC and the FCA, this is your starter for ten. Or perhaps he means Tesco should include all its customers in the decision making when it comes to deciding whose crisp packets to stack their shelves with?

"Leaders have to fix the present social contract. Moreover, they must also design the contracts necessary for the post-industrial age, with its new features of circular and shared economies". We can only thank the Lord that Thomas Hobbes and Jean-Jacques Rousseau are not around to read this bizarre hijacking of their great works!

Indeed, "the time has come to rethink the economic and social norms by which we measure societal progress." I'm not sure I've come across the term "societal progress" before but I expect China's president XI Jinping can enlighten us when he attends the Davos bash next week. No doubt Schwab will meet with a receptive Chinese audience when he goes on to remind them, and all others present that "leaders have to create and engage in agile and informal cooperation platforms required for the political, economic, social and technological context of the 21st century. Leadership always comprises stewardship for the world as a whole-holistically taking care of humankind and nature." Good luck with that lot tripping off the translators' tongues.

There is so much more but by now I expect you are almost ready to run screaming to the pub. But permit me just one more pass at the Schwab sheet: "The world is fundamentally transforming technologically, economically, socially and politically. The ongoing transformation needs to be shaped by appropriate policies and institutions. There are no simple, ready-made solutions. What we urgently need are pragmatic and future-orientated actions, even in the form of small steps, to provide positive narratives."

Can a transformation be shaped by a policy? What are these magical policies and institutions? I thought all actions by definition take place in the future. Can steps provide narratives? Give me strength. Davos man has for some years been susceptible to disappearing up his own hind quarters. Schwab's mangled outpouring looks set to take them well into that "unmapped territory". Time gentlemen, please.

16 March 2017

With Charlotte Hogg resigning from Bank of England, all that's left is to sack Hammond and Carney

Thank goodness the sub optimal players at the heart of our financial establishment – like Charlotte Hogg, Hammond and Carney – are beginning to feel the heat.

First out the door has been Charlotte Hogg who at least grasped the problem of "do as I say, not as I do". Unsurprisingly this seems to have evaded the mental capacity of Carney who rejected her first offer to resign.

But Carney will shortly have his own career to worry about. His opposite number over in the US, Janet Yellen, is preparing to embark on a series of interest rate rises starting with one this week.

Writing in the FT on Tuesday the well-respected Mohamed El-Erian made the following observation: "Look for this week's Federal Open Market Committee meeting to be remembered as constituting a serious attempt – the most serious so far – by the Fed to leave behind the 'lower for longer' paradigm that has been a key part of its unconventional monetary policy.

"Success, however, is not something that the central bank can deliver on its own. Its wellbeing, and more importantly that of the economy and markets, requires that politicians in the US, Europe, Japan and China also step up to their economic governance responsibilities."

Here Carny has a problem all of his own making as his idiotic interest rate cut, made thanks to his misreading of Brexit, has him facing entirely the wrong way. Unfortunately the immediate consequence of his own ineptitude is to have turned Sterling into a smouldering ruin. Has he the guts now to follow the path so clearly laid out by El-Erian? If he fails to respond by the end of the month then we can only hope Theresa May invites the hapless man to tea at Downing Street to consider his position.

Which brings me to Hammond. Now that the prime minister has wisely insisted he ditches the self-employed NI increase, she should follow through by showing him the door. As I said in last week's City Grump we cannot have a laughing stock of a chancellor when it comes to squaring up to Article 50.

She must show she means business by demonstrating she will not tolerate slipshod policy making by our financial establishment. That means saying goodbye to Hammond and Carney. Mrs May has no alternative.

24 March 2017

Does it matter that our ex-chancellor ran into the arms of wealthy new bosses? Yes, it does

The former Chancellor George Osborne has brought shame to his former office, the highest in the land after that of Prime Minister. Most citizens would wish this extraordinarily responsible position to be occupied by men and women of unimpeachable integrity and moral standards – in this case someone not cut from the same cloth as Osborne.

To fill the role of chancellor we look for men and women who cannot be influenced in their lives by expensive baubles dangled in front of them or by being drawn into private powerful commercial concerns. By accepting £650,000 per annum from Black Rock and the editorship of the London Evening Standard, Osborne has driven a coach and horses through such principals. His selfishness has yet again besmirched political life in Britain today. Is it any wonder that so many of the electorate look upon Westminster with disgust and contempt?

When I last looked Black Rock was a fund management business. What does our ex-Chancellor know about that? He would no more know how to run an ETF than drive a grand prix car. Actually, as Channel 4 reported this week, Osborne's financial probity is currently under scrutiny for allegedly having a hand in encouraging State-owned RBS to cut back the balance sheet by pushing scores of SMEs into the now notorious Global Restructuring Group (GRG) and then onwards into the "bad bank".

The only possible reasons for Black Rock's eagerness to have him climb aboard is (1) to exploit his political connections and (2) shelling out £650k in relation to a fee income is miniscule (that old question "yes but where are the clients' yachts?" comes to mind). Even that hotbed of political back scratching, the EU, got very angry indeed when José Manuel Barroso flew into the arms of Goldman Sachs. Why aren't we just as angry over Osborne's appointment?

There is of course the Advisory Committee on Business Appointments (Acoba), which was set up to approve, or not, posts applied for by ex-government ministers and senior civil servants. Clearly Osborne thinks Acoba can be treated with contempt (he might be right as it approved the Black Rock appointment) as he hasn't even bothered to seek permission for his appointment to the Evening Standard's editorship.

As Private Eye observed he has delivered an "unequivocal two fingers to them". Indeed Osborne has form here with his Northern Powerhouse chairmanship, when Acoba noted "The Committee wrote to Osborne about his appointment with the Northern Powerhouse Partnership, noting that it is unable to offer retrospective advice on applications that have already been announced".

Appointing Osborne as editor of a major newspaper is akin to appointing Len McCluskey editor of Vogue magazine. It is an insult to its professional journalists and must leave much of its 1.7m readers wondering if they have entered an Alice in Wonderland novel. Again surely such an appointment can only make sense on the basis that the Standard's owners expect Osborne to exercise effective political influence on their behalf?

Is it ethical or morally right that an ex-Chancellor can fall into such positions or are we descending into the ways of a Banana Republic? Time for the Mother of Parliaments to bring its home grown children back into line.

CHAPTER 2

CAPITALISM
IN THE RAW

"Bad economics teaches that computers can design markets. Good economics teaches that markets can design computers."

Jakub Bożydar Wiśniewski

"In short, if you are using a shovel to dig yourself into a hole, a credit card company will be happy to give you a backhoe."

Jason G. Miller

I have spent most of my working life involved with stock markets. Functioning well they are fascinating creatures. Individual investors and institutional ones come together in constant real time to decide what value to put on a company. When times are good that company can raise capital for expansion and when times are bad that company must make a case for fresh capital to help it along. If it can't, then it may fail. Capitalism in the raw.

But, and it is a big but, the market is not always like that. These are the days of computer driven, algorithmic, buying and selling. These are the days of large scale passive index investment funds that are programmed to follow a market index and nothing more. The result is that human beings making human decisions are now often thin on the ground.

To paraphrase the legendary American stockbroker, Bernard Baruch, yes stock markets often make fools of us all. Witness Baruch's client, a certain Winston Churchill who lost his proverbial shirt in the 1929 crash. But that is all the reason to respect this most capitalist of mechanisms and the City Grumps here do just that.

And so we come to debt. We live in a sea of it. Our children are "blooded" in its embrace when they attend university, leaving there with at least £50,000 owing to the State. Banks, on average, lend out ten times their capital base. Andrew McNally in his book, "Debtonator", calculated that if you expressed the world's debt in one dollar bill and laid them end to end they would stretch to Mars and back fifty times. Recently the Bank of England and the FCA calculated that nine out of every ten pounds of outstanding credit card debt was owed by people who were also in the red two years earlier. You'd expect the City Grump to have a go at skewering the debt monster and you are right.

17 August, 2010

Bank debt: the end of an era?

Every day now in every paper the discussions rage on over bank lending to SMEs. The debt junkies can't quite believe that the era of funding their businesses through a nice and easy bank loan is over. Well, it's cold turkey time, ladies and gentleman.

Surely by now it must be evident to the readers of Real Business that the high-street banks would prefer to turn their back on the small business world. If you can ever get them to be candid they will admit they no longer have the internal infrastructure to cope with lending £0.5m here, £1m there to thousands and thousands of little customers. Unless, of course you want a mortgage and even then, with valuations heading downhill again, I wouldn't count on it.

At the risk of making myself deeply unpopular, I think turning the debt trap sorry, tap, off is a healthy development. It may feel like cold turkey but businesses will be better for it.

The goal for every small business should be to finance long-term capital through equity. By all means use trade debtor finance but stop at that. How can you access equity? Start by writing a coherent business plan. If you can't do that why on earth should anyone believe you are competent to build a business?

Of course in your early days it is highly unlikely you will be able to access equity from the public markets such as AIM and PLUS or indeed from the private equity houses. But there are other avenues. For example, did you know that Luke Johnson, the well-known small cap investor, ex of Pizza Express, and weekly FT columnist on entrepreneurship, recently bought a 27 per cent stake in Beer & Partners, one of our biggest business angel networks? His logic is that, "angel investment is the only realistic option for early-stage companies. Currently banks are barely open for business or tend to offer loans on unattractive terms, so the need for equity capital (for early-stage businesses) is greater than ever. Since current low interest rates give savers such poor returns, more and more angel investors are emerging that have a strong appetite for direct investment in small companies".

Then, of course, don't forget friends and family. If you feel confident enough that your business will be a success but you need capital, why not raise some equity from these sources? If you are not confident, scared of putting together a plan, or simply fearful of asking, why should anyone bother with you?

Ask any addict and he/she will tell you that you need discipline to kick the habit. Wean yourself off the bank and enjoy a long life with equity.

9 September, 2011

The first casualty of (financial) war is truth

The war being waged by politicians and bankers to combat 40 years of profligate overspending by western governments and households is seeing us subjected to an endless procession of lies, disinformation and cover-ups.

Let's start with the macro scene. The best summation I have seen of the sovereign debt cover-up comes from Jerome Booth, head of research at fund manager Ashmore. I quote: "There is a dead body on the kitchen floor, and blood everywhere. It is dealt with in different ways by different nationalities. The British find it hard to cope with, but try to clear up the mess as quickly as possible. The Europeans cover the body with a sheet and agree to deal with it later – but the sheet isn't big enough and the blood keeps seeping out, so they get another sheet, and another. Initially, the Germans keep their corner of the kitchen spotless, and have plenty of floor-cleaning equipment, but are reluctant to mop up the stains in other areas. The Americans place the corpse in a chair, give it a cup of coffee and try to engage it in conversation."

In the fog of war, dear reader, the only chance you have of keeping some sort of grip on reality is to summon up the most precious tool you use in your business life: common sense.

Common sense tells you that clearing this mess up will be expensive for everyone on the planet (some catastrophically so) and for our "leaders" to tell us otherwise is just resorting to the usual wartime trick of attempting to boost morale.

On the home front, our Chancellor is engaging in just such a morale boosting excercise, as this week he has been doing the rounds saying that we, in our nice, tight little island, "can remain masters of our own destiny".

This is rubbish.

Terry Smith, chief executive of Tullett Prebon, in a letter to the FT this week (headed: "We have to be told just how bad the situation is") draws attention to all the disinformation being pedalled by the Tories on how they are getting our debt under control. In an attempt to make a clear and unambiguous statement about the actual debt the UK is carrying, his company has just sent to every member of parliament a tin can emblazoned with the real UK debt commitment – that's £3,589bn folks – so they can see what they are metaphorically "kicking down the road" with their present policies.

Occasionally, of course, when a leader is no longer in power, he/she lets out a few truths – as Alastair Darling has done in his recently published book. Or Lord Lawson when he said recently that the single currency is "among the most irresponsible initiatives of the post-war world".

Actually, some of the consequences of the "Euro deception" were underlined by surprisingly honest remarks from the CEO of Deutsche Bank, Josef Ackermann: "It is an open secret that numerous European banks would not survive having to revalue sovereign debt held on the banking book at market value."

Sadly (pathetically?), back on the home front, our bankers are still attempting to derail the expected recommendation of the Vickers Commission to split off their so-called investment banking activities.

The lies and disinformation have reached fever pitch. Investment banking should have been relabelled "investment gaming". They are gaming the system and, as a result, their activities are dangerous, counterproductive and hence should have no place in sensible banking.

Remarkably, in his same speech, Ackermann went on to say: "We have a financial industry that is still not really providing convincing answers to the questions about the meaningfulness of many financial products and trading in securities... we must, in my opinion, check all our work in all our areas thoroughly again to ascertain whether we prioritise our genuine tasks as servants of the real economic needs."

A pity, therefore, that our own bankers continue to lie when it comes to the simplest of things such as Project Merlin's lending to SMEs.

Here the bankers maintain their lending commitments are on track, even though the Bank of England has pointed out the figures are misleading because they show the credit made available to business not the credit actually used.

Here, on the frontline, may I try and transmit the following message back to the command and control bunkers: All over the western world, there are thousands of companies and individuals sitting on cash. In order to kickstart growth, you need to provide incentives for them to invest. The most cost-effective incentives are targeted tax breaks (eg: in the UK, no CGT payable on investment in small companies). Do this, stop considering throwing more money at quantitative easing and the like, and then we might start believing in you again.

5 October, 2011

Osborne's "credit easing" scheme: hoodwinking voters

George Osborne's proposals for a "credit easing" scheme for small businesses, announced at the Conservative Party conference, is a PR triumph – but not much else.

At this week's party conference the Chancellor said "you cannot borrow your way out of debt" but can SMEs borrow their way to growth?

Politicians love to be able to announce something new. It captures the media's attention, catches most commentators sufficiently off guard to head off any immediate penetrating questions, and means the caravan can move seemlessly onto something else at conference the next day.

So it was not hard for Osborne to win some plaudits for his idea on the government standing behind packaged-up tradeable loans to small companies.

I congratulate him on his PR triumph but not much else.

I did, however, find two very sensible immediate comments. One was from Andrew Cave at the Federation of Small Businesses who said "small businesses in this country have no experience of issuing bonds so there's a hell of a lot of work to be done to look into the details of how this might function".

The other was from Lombard in the FT who, having pointed out the creation of a new securitisations market would be tricky and time consuming (more on that later), went on to say "the admirable curmudgeons who own better small companies have a long history of declining to borrow, even when lenders want them to. That is why the SME sector had net cash on deposit for much of the overleveraged noughties… Small companies will invest when it benefits them, not when it benefits the UK."

These comments go to the heart of the problem, which is the continuing poor advice from the Treasury. Alistair Darling recounted, in his recent book, the comment from his Permanent Secretary Nick Macpherson that when he became Chancellor "there were only about three people (at the Treasury) who had experienced a recession".

In my experience, this all-important organ of government is filled with bright 24 year olds, fresh from their MBA courses, long on theory and short on everything else.

Somewhat to my amusement, this was confirmed to me the other day when I had a meeting with a think tank boss who said "you are absolutely right, I was one of those people"!

Combine this febrile environment with a 40-year-old Chancellor lacking in business experience and you have the ideal breeding ground for half-baked ideas while ignoring the lessons of hundreds of years of history.

Those lessons tell you that if you want to put in place lasting capital foundations for companies, you do it largely with equity – not debt. Indeed for the past 60 or so years we have built up a comprehensive infrastructure that, despite the ravages of recession, remains perfectly capable of advising SMEs on equity fund raising and the requirements of the associated capital markets.

As Andrew Cave and Lombard point out, no such apparatus exist for small company bonds.

In order for an effective capital-raising mechanism to function, you have to make sure there is an active secondary market. This existed when a previous Conservative Chancellor, Ken Clarke, made all capital gains from investing and trading in AIM and PLUS-listed shares CGT free. It is not beyond the capability (or, sadly, maybe it is?) of the Treasury to restore this for all companies with a market cap of, say, less than £50m.

This would attract a large number of investors back into this vital area for the British economy, thus boosting growth and improving tax revenues.

But why revive a infrastructure that works when it is so much more fun to hoodwink voters with something new?

If Osborne and his band of young helpers dig a little deeper into the business world, they'll find the objectives of the equity holder are vey different to that of the bondholder. The loan provider is not concerned about the growth of the SME. All he wants to know is that the company is generating sufficient cash to be able to pay him back at the end of the loan period. The equity holder is interested in the long-term future of the company, as growth will make his stake more valuable.

Now, which of those two would you rather have aboard your business?

30 July, 2012

Everything is awful. (Time to be bullish)

After five years of being told I was a miserable moaning minnie, now everyone everywhere is in despair. That's good news, time to get back into our equity markets.

It has been a long wait but at last all is gloom apart, of course, from the short-term splendid palliative that is the Olympic Games for our armchair enthusiasts. From the "greatest show on earth" to the worst. So:

- UK GDP numbers are dire.
- Osborne is being called "a Chancellor on work experience".
- Cameron says it will be 2020 before we emerge from the financial swamp

- Our banks are out of control.
- The Financial Times entitles an article on AIM, "Pond life" and suggests all companies with a market cap of less than £10m should leave.
- Pension funds and insurance companies hold the lowest percentage of equities for forty years.
- Everyone with more than two brain cells now admits that Euroland is finished in its current form.
- The US is politically paralysed as the traditional Punch and Judy fest, known as the Presidential election trail, gets under way.
- World food prices are going to rocket as corn yields, etc, are biblically awful.
- China is slowing down.
- The Middle East becomes scarier by the day.
- South American economies are heading south and then there is that crazy lady running Argentina.
- Oh and lastly, there is the frightening possibility that arch FSA opportunist, Lord Turner, might talk his way into the Governorship of the BoE.

In short everything is awful. Even our very own irrepressible Charlie Mullins says the Olympics is bad for business. But this is great. You see when everyone has given up that means, to put it in the context of equity markets, everyone who was going to sell has by now done so. When there are no sellers left then, guess what, share prices go up!

More than 200 years ago the founder of the Rothschild banking dynasty said: "buy when there is blood on the streets". Well there is plenty of the modern-day equivalent all around us. Over the 21st century, most stock prices of companies at best are back to where they started or are substantially lower. The City Grump has indeed put his money where his mouth with a recent and not immaterial purchase of stock in one of our better run brewery cum pub companies. Come on in. The water (or should that be beer?) is lovely.

21 August, 2012

Now would be a good time to reset both our rules and our values (part I)

Our financial elites are running out of answers; it's not surprising that politicians are wobbling with them.

Reshaping finance for a new season is the subtitle of James Featherby's seminal new book, 'Of Markets and Men'. I make no apology for making over this City Grump article, and the next, to some truly excellent extracts from it.

In part one, below, Featherby highlights how debt is enslaving us all, how quantitative easing should be used for putting an end to the unhealthy power of banks and bondholders, and what we should be replacing that debt with to finance employment and a more productive and happier society. Time for a reset! Time for a revolution in thinking!

"Government debt is no more than a promise made by the government to the bond markets to tax the citizens of tomorrow to meet the promises made by government to the tax payers of today. Politicians have not learnt how to put a cap on their welfare promises and are always tempted to kick the can of repayment down the road towards tomorrow. The government cannot issue equity, only debt.

"In a season when governments are anxious to fund themselves, some see more than a coincidence in the changing regulatory landscape that requires pension funds, insurance companies and banks to hold an increasing level of debt and in fiscal policies that maintain downward pressure on interest rates. However, one cannot get the better of bond markets forever, and at some point the markets may decline to continue funding ever decreasing yields and ever decreasing sovereign debt qualities.

"Lawrence Summers, a former United States Secretary of the Treasury, sums up the current overriding objectives of governments,

'Government has no higher responsibility than insuring economies have an adequate level of demand. Without growing demand, there is no prospect of sustained growth, let alone a significant fall in joblessness. And without either of these there is no chance of reducing debt-to-income ratios.'

"How sad that our collective dreams have been reduced by the political and economic establishment down to a simple desire to see us consume in order to reduce debt-to-income ratios. The lack of choice that this agenda suggests denotes modern day slavery: work simply to pay debts. Excessive debt has imprisoned our paradigms and our possibilities.

"Excessive debt produces inflation, injustice and the modern day equivalent of slavery, where the economic futures of men and women are committed to a debt they cannot repay. Excessive debt centralises power, fuels speculation and turns others into a means not an end. The current economic climate can leave us in no doubt that we need substantially less debt. Government reforms to date might or might not make banks safer. They have done little, however, to address the quantum of debt. Reducing the level of personal, corporate and national debt will make our personal, corporate and national finances more stable, more equitable, more sustainable, and more enjoyable.

"Our forefathers were cuter than we might have imagined. They recognised that debt had a tendency to enslave both economically and psychologically. Even before banks were creating money, and debt, on the current industrial scale and even before debt based economies were fashionable because of the previous distaste for lending money with interest, our forefathers recognised that every now and then it was necessary to step in and cut the Gordian knot if poverty and slavery, including the sense of alienation and hopelessness to which they give rise, were not to become permanently institutionalised.

"Simply cancelling debts in the modern economy would cause too much chaos: the insolvencies amongst those to whom the debts were owed, and amongst those to whom they in turn owed debts, would cause widespread problems. A further alternative, at least on a national basis, may be a variant on the quantitative easing (QE) theme.

"At present QE appears to be boosting bank reserves without resolving wider problems. Instead QE could be used, and effectively without creating more debt, to give money directly to every private person in the country. This would be on condition that it was used to repay their debts, and that those receiving payments (for example banks) in turn repaid their debts (for example to bondholders).

"Those with no debts would still receive the gift and, although not central in the scheme, they could be encouraged to spend the money in ways that boosted the economy: preferably through investing in businesses that create employment or are looking to increase productivity. A beneficial by-product would be the shrinking of bank balance sheets back towards their pre-credit boom size. It was a sleight of hand that produced money/debt. Maybe it will take another to reduce it.

"Debt finances the familiar since the familiar normally has an asset base that can be provided as security. It does not finance innovation since innovation offers little by way of security. In a knowledge and service based economy such as ours this is a particular shortcoming.

"The pressure on profitability is, among other things, likely to spur the investment banks on in their promotion of the debt capital markets as an alternative to traditional bank lending, since the investment banks are the controllers of the bond issuance process and can earn fees accordingly.

"Only 12 investment banks control 58 per cent by volume of the global bond issuance market. They are positioning themselves such that only they have the necessary knowledge, international relationships and underwriting strength to act as book runners on major debt capital market issues. "The control by an even smaller group of global banks of certain derivatives that accompany bond issues is even stronger. An oligopoly is growing over one of the world's major sources of finance.

"A signpost towards a lower debt economy would be the abolition of the favourable tax treatment currently given to debt, which in practice results in a tax subsidy being given to one set of taxpayers (mostly business borrowers) by another set of taxpayers (everyone else)...The favourable tax treatment given to debt disincentivises equity investment, which is more stable and risk sharing.

"The UK banks have persuaded us that we must not endanger growth by restricting the ability of banks to lend. This argument would hold considerably less water if equity investment were able to compete on a level playing field. This would be less inflationary and would lead to greater willingness to invest in productivity and innovation...Equity investments could be further encouraged through a more favourable CGT regime for equity securities compared to debt securities, including by gradually reducing the level of tax payable on gains the longer equity securities are held.

"The key to kicking the habit of excessive debt is to believe that it is worthwhile and that it is possible. That creates the space needed to imagine things differently, and it provides the energy to find solutions to the objections of those who say it cannot be done. Surely if anything proves that taking money/debt out of the system, and of creating a system in which money/debt cannot accumulate as it has before, it is the events of the last few years. Those preserving the status quo are the ones who need to prove they are not living in the asylum."

22 January 2016

The bull in the China shop: Money managers short on history and long on panic

The money managers have started 2016 in a blue funk – but most are too young to remember what kicked off at the end of the 1980s and the fact that, with the exception of the instigator, we weren't then doomed to years of economic gloom.

In 1988 some clever statistician worked out that the valuation of the land surrounding the Japanese Emperor's palace in Tokyo was higher than all the real estate in California. Shortly after this revelation the wheels started coming off the Japanese economy and its GDP has, relative to what went before for several decades, flat-lined ever since.

China now has 12 per cent of the world's GDP, similar to Japan's share in 1990 which was also 12 per cent. In common with the China of today Japan back then was propelled by massive investment, an explosive credit growth, a huge trade surplus and an overvalued currency. Its stock markets had become the plaything of the gambling private investor. Japanese bosses indulged themselves in a massive buying spree of foreign assets – everything from art to American steel companies. Now it is the turn of the Chinese to be seen to be just as profligate.

In the same way as we are told China is the great God of all things economic, it is amusing to recall in the 1980s Japan was donning the very same mantle. And did the world stop when it realised the Emperor was not wearing the equivalent of California? No it didn't. Our young money managers are short on history and long on panic. If it was the other way round they would soon realise the world doesn't live in an economic hegemony for very long. It moves on.

As if on cue, our planet's most savvy company, Apple, is reported in the Financial Times' 21st January edition, to be shifting its focus to India as China's smartphone market slows down. "Apple views India as the most likely replacement for the booming sales in China that have powered its rise in recent years," it stated. "Apple may soon begin to manufacture in India. Foxconn, the Taiwanese contract manufacturer that makes most iPhones announced plans to set up in India last year."

I wonder how many are presently worrying themselves silly in Davos about what Chinese flat-lining is going to do to their career prospects, and whether they are entertaining the thought that India could be where it's at quite soon now. Of course, Professor Henry Mintzberg described the Davos gathering as the event "where the people who spend all year causing our problems take a few days pretending to fix them".

Most of those strutting round this Swiss mountain emporium are paid handsomely. If you added up the remuneration of all present there, I suspect the total would now buy all of the Japanese's Emperor's land together with much choice real estate in California as well. Back in September 2013 I wrote a City

Grump entitled "The Cancer of Socialism is out of Remission – Why?" I argued "Socialism spreads when it is able to feed off highly visible blatant abuses of financial privilege and right now conditions for its destructive ingress are near perfect. Why? Because there is an intolerable mismatch of the rewards paid to managers at the top of their particular trees and those struggling to cling to the branches."

I pointed to KPMG's 2012 survey of FTSE 100 Directors' basic salaries, which found that "the average CEO was given over £800k, while other executive directors gained approximately £500k last year. FTSE 250 equivalents gained a mere £450k and £300k respectively. In all 350 companies, KPMG recorded that when you add in bonuses, share incentive schemes, etc, etc, these ladies and gentleman trebled their remuneration."

I said these people were often referred to as fat cats, but "I would prefer to call them sloths. Google tells me that 'after consuming a large meal two-thirds of the sloth's bodyweight will consist of the contents of its stomach'. Contrast then, these enormous feasts with the diet that the rest of us have been asked to go on for the last five years following previous excess, then it is plain as a pikestaff why Socialists are going to get a hearing between now and the next election."

That was in 2012 and nothing has changed for the better. Indeed we now have Jeremy Corbyn drawing attention to the spectacular financial rewards that are being paid out to those at or near the top of our larger companies and other institutions. Thanks to this excess, the hard left in the UK and the hard right in the US (Donald Trump) are making all the running. Ultimately this state of affairs is much more damaging to Western economies than any slowdown in China. As an old business colleague of mine said: "Too many financiers and big business chiefs are trying to live like Yusupov princes." Will anyone in Davos take note and take action?

7 March 2016

AIM must be set free from any LSE mega-merger

With "exchanges" clearly seeing providing the facilities to list and trade equities as of ever diminishing importance, it doesn't take much of a mental leap to realise at the monthly board meetings of the directors of Mega Exchange, AIM will never be given any agenda airtime at all.

At a conference in December 2009, Paul Volcker, ex Federal Reserve chairman, said: "I wish that somebody would give me some shred of neutral evidence about the relationship between financial innovation recently and the growth of the economy, just one shred of information. A few years ago I happened to be at a conference of business people, not financial people, and I was making a presentation. The conference was being addressed by a very vigorous young investment banker from London who was explaining to all these older executives how their companies would be dust if they did not realise the joys of financial innovation and financial engineering, and that they had better get with it.

"I was listening to this and I found myself sitting next to one of the inventors of financial engineering who I did not know, but I knew who he was and that he had won a Nobel Prize, and I nudged him and asked what all the financial engineering does for the economy and what it does for productivity. Much to my surprise he leaned over and whispered in my ear that it does nothing. I asked him what it did do and he said that it moves around the rents in the financial system and besides that it was a lot of intellectual fun."

When the London Stock Exchange (LSE) falls into the arms of Deutsche Borse or ICE (the Intercontinental Exchange that owns the New York Stock Exchange and others), approaching three quarters of the merged business' revenue will come from serving the derivative markets that Volcker refers to above. Only one quarter will come from cash equity markets, meaning equities bought and sold through their exchanges and of this AIM will provide an almost microscopic amount of revenue.

I make no comment on the efficacy of the LSE deciding to annoy the inestimable Volcker even further but only to note it is a business and like any business it will go where it believes that it can make the most profit. This being the case, you cannot get away from the fact that these "exchanges" clearly see providing the facilities to list and trade equities as of ever diminishing importance. It doesn't take much of a mental leap to realise at the monthly board meetings of the directors of Mega Exchange, AIM will never be given any agenda airtime at all.

It is not difficult to work out how this will make the, by then, almost invisible AIM staff feel. In a word, lousy. The capable staff will leave and then it won't be long before that whole market withers on the vine.

AIM is of no consequence to this brave new world of global exchanges but it is of significance and importance to small company capital formation. Last year AIM marked its 20th anniversary and over that time it has raised £90bn of equity for its companies. This is a fantastic achievement and one that must not be ignored by those charged with the task of examining proposed tie ups between the LSE, Deutsche Borse, ICE, or indeed any other exchange.

I would bet a pound to a pinch of salt that right now 95 per cent of companies on AIM have not thought about the consequences of what is written here and most of AIM's advisor community hasn't yet woken up either. With the honourable exception of Anthony Hilton in last week's Evening Standard, none of the major media outlets have looked at this issue.

Add this all up and it is extremely unlikely it has come to the attention of the relevant government ministries, meaning the Treasury and the Business, Industry and Skills department. This state of affairs cannot be allowed to continue.

The solution is obvious. AIM must be set free and this can of course be achieved by our Government making it a condition of any LSE mega merger that AIM is carved out as an independent entity. Then it can attract the right calibre of staff to ensure a flourishing future for that vital small company equity capital raising in the UK. Then it can be at the forefront of new developments such as the possibility of bringing crowdfunding into AIM stock issues. In reality the Mega Exchange alternative will result in the closure of AIM.

What can you do? You should write to your MP, Sajid Javid Minister of State at the BIS, and to Harriet Baldwin at the Treasury (she is the minister responsible for the City) and tell them that unless AIM is set free this country will lose a much needed, well established, smaller company resource. The City Grump will do his best but he needs your help!

Let me leave the last word to Paul Volcker, the wise head who served five US Presidents: "The most important financial innovation that I have seen the past 20 years is the automatic teller machine, that really helps people and prevents visits to the bank and it is a real convenience. How many other innovations can you tell me of that have been as important to the individual as the automatic teller machine, which is more of a mechanical innovation than a financial one?

"I have found very little evidence that vast amounts of innovation in financial markets in recent years has had a visible effect on the productivity of the economy, maybe you can show me that I am wrong".

CHAPTER 3

REGULATION IS FROM MARS, INVESTMENT IS FROM VENUS

If you can't understand why someone is doing something, look at the consequences of their actions, whatever they might be, and then infer the motivations from their consequences"

Jordan. B. Peterson.

A recurring theme during the City Grump years has been the interaction between investment, regulation and that which is being invested in and regulated. Like the eternal triangle the three parties can't seem to live with each other but can't live without each other either. One of the earliest City Grumps (April 2010) argued that if our schools' curriculum spent time in giving our teenagers a strong financial education then the dead hand of regulation would diminish as investment became easier for everyone to understand, scams easier to spot and financial greed harder to get away with. Sadly the financial regulator has little incentive to improve the lifeblood of the nation whether it is in the shape of small company investing, equity capital or what goes into our pension pots, or indeed bringing those at the heart of RBS, HBOS and other banking scandals to justice. Instead the FCA prefers to concentrate on staying in Brussels' good books, staying away from Westminster scrutiny, and turning the compliance industry into Britain's fastest growing business sector.

As ever our politicians are pretty financially clueless. How many MPs have actually run businesses or built up investments? Pitifully few. Now that the scourge of regulatory ineptitude and financial crime, Andrew Tyrie, has gone from the Treasury Select Committee to be replaced by Nicky Morgan, whose main claim to fame seems to be complaining about the cost of Mrs May's trousers, don't expect things to get better.

27 April, 2010

Education, not regulation

The consensual response to the global financial road crash of 2008/9 is "let's have more regulation!". A better approach would be to take up Mr Blair's discarded slogan of "education, education, education".

Education, not regulation – Educate our children about financial housekeeping.

Regulation is bound to fail on almost any number of fronts but let me highlight a few obvious ones.

First, capitalism. Financial institutions will always be able to afford to employ people smarter than regulators, thus the authorities will forever be doomed to be behind the curve of the next dangerous financial wheeze.

Second, practitioners will concentrate on following the letter of regulation, not the spirit. This is a great game for many and keeps endless lawyers and other expensively educated people in fine fettle.

Third, cross-continent regulatory co-operation sounds nice but is totally impossible to achieve. Why, UK and US Intelligence cannot even co-ordinate on the surveillance of al-Qaeda recruits! What chance do the suits at the FSA, SEC etc have?

If we are to have any hope of achieving lasting financial probity, we need to grab the populace when it is young. If we continue to rely on simply learning rules and regulations then, when Janet and John enter the workplace, we will be continuously shutting doors after horses have bolted.

Instead we must instil in our children the virtues of financial responsibility and integrity at an early age because then we give them the best possible chance of becoming useful citizens in their careers.

In among the usual toe-curlingly awful television ads from the high-street banks (to my mind, the Halifax regularly carries off the prize for the most cringeworthy), I saw one recently from Nat West, featuring some of its bright-eyed and bushy-tailed staff going into schools and teaching children the basic financial facts of life.

The irony that its parent, RBS, had to be given the biggest financial bailout in UK government history seems to have been lost on those responsible for the ad – but c'est la vie!

Perhaps the necessity of educating our children about sound financial housekeeping is finally beginning to get through. I do hope so. Maybe then there will be fewer in the workforce who regard it as a God-given right that they should have a large mortgage, be able to educate their kids privately, take expensive holidays every year and so on. Then SMEs will be able to afford to employ talented staff, who don't need absurdly large uneconomic salaries to finance their over-inflated and irresponsible lifestyle.

18 May, 2010

The big bad corporates

I know small companies are in my blood – and I understand big companies will always command the higher profile. But recent events yet again show why big is ugly and small is beautiful.

All rookie entrants to the City are taught that big companies are generally blue-chip investments and small companies are inherently risky. Indeed, those arbiters of regulatory fashion, the FSA, are very keen that private clients should be alerted to the dangers of putting money into small caps. Events, dear boy, suggest otherwise as, yet again, the heavy brigade lumbers into the ditch.

This time around it is BP and the Pru in the frame. The former with a highly embarrassing oil leak and the latter over a painful misjudgement with the FSA over approval for its mega Asian deal.

What do these events have in common? I would suggest senior management failings. Why do these happen? I would suggest that big companies, by their nature, only have so-called professional managers and, more often than not, these managers have no close attachment or feel for their companies. Creative energy therefore gets channelled into self-advancement through office politics, resulting in the management eye frequently being off the ball at crucial moments.

The scene is usually very different in small companies. Here, senior managers are often the creators of the company and, naturally, have a deep attachment to it. In these circumstances, crucial decisions are taken with the benefit of a level of knowledge and interest, which is just not there in those big uglies.

Mix into the above ingredients the phenomena that small companies have to manage their balance sheets prudently (as banks instinctively prefer lending to the so-called blue chips – remind me, what happened to GEC?) then you begin to wonder why a portfolio of small-cap investments is regarded as inherently more risky than one populated by behemoths.

The time has surely come for the small-company universe to take heed of the new political landscape that is being created before our eyes. After all, the attention given by government and media to the constituents of the FTSE 100 is massively disproportionate to the number of people employed by small companies. Proportional representation would suggest, at the very least, a Minister for Small Companies at the cabinet table!

31 August, 2010

FSA: No friend of the SME community

On a wall in the reception area of the FSA's Canary Wharf HQ are the words to Bob Dylan's song Positively 4th Street: "You got a lotta nerve to say you are my friend. When I was down you just stood there grinning. You got a lotta nerve to say you got a helping hand to lend. You just want to be on the side that's winning." Some would say this shows the FSA has a sense of humour. Others would point out that the words of this famous song appear to chime with its attitude to small caps in general.

This became painfully obvious when chatting to those who intend to respond to the government's Green Paper on financing smaller companies. One of them highlighted the FSA's official description of AIM and PLUS Quoted companies, saying:

"Penny Shares. What are they? This tends to be a general term for shares on junior stock markets and unlisted shares. They tend to be very high risk, can be difficult to sell in some cases and may be quoted in pence, hence the name."

No doubt companies such as Majestic Wine, Datacash (now being bid for by Mastercard), and Shepherd Neame (oldest brewer in the UK) are thrilled to find themselves labelled as "penny shares" by this FSA document. Should we ignore the recent Sunday Times Money article that pointed out the FTSE AIM Index went up 21 per cent in the past 12 months compared to nine per cent for the FTSE 100? Also, just in passing, did anyone point out to this FSA scribe that all UK shares are quoted in pence?!

In a few ill-chosen but highly revealing words, the UK's regulatory authority shows itself to be no friend of the small company community. This malevolence has simply got to stop and I would urge all those who read this column to say so in your response to the Green Paper.

If all this wasn't bad enough for those toiling away on the small company scene, then along comes the FSA's latest creation, the Standard Listing section of the FSA-administered Full List. Among other delights, companies can be admitted to the Standard List with no 12-month working capital statement, no sponsor or nominated adviser (nomad) and no shareholder approval requirement for significant or related-party transactions. I am indebted to Steptoe and Johnson LLP, for the following: "The new Standard Listing regime may... fundamentally weaken investor protection. It is feared that companies may gravitate towards the easier option of a Standard Listing on LSE's main market. There is the possibility that nomads might encourage less reputable clients to shift up to a Standard Listing, thereby releasing the nomad of its legal responsibilities. Indeed, it is conceivable that a financial advisory firm that did not achieve nomad status because it fell short of regulatory requirements could now bypass this rejection and float a company on the market anyway via a Standard Listing."

The FSA calls AIM and PLUS Quoted "penny share markets". What does that make the Standard List? Where do they point out that it could easily be the highest risk UK equity market of all?

Dylan's song on the FSA's wall goes on to say: "You see me on the street, you always act surprised. You say: 'How are you? Good luck' – but you don't mean it. When you know as well as me you'd rather see me paralysed, why don't you just come out once and scream it?"

Those of us working in the junior markets know what Bob means.

9 September, 2010

Triumph over the FSA

You know victory is yours when the other side (in this case, the Financial Services Authority) quietly and surreptitiously changes course.

It's very interesting to see that, a few days after my City Grump column highlighted that the FSA's website definition of penny shares included all companies on AIM and PLUS Quoted, all reference to AIM and PLUS Quoted is suddenly removed by them!

Someone high up in the FSA's North Colonnade Tower HQ must have realised that their political masters would be none too happy to read that the organisation was making life unnecessarily difficult for the small-company community, especially at a time when banks have turned unfriendly as well.

Talking of banks, it is equally distressing to see that the FSA seems to be sticking the knife into small-company lending as well. On Tuesday, it was reported in the Daily Telegraph that Steve Pateman, head of Santander UK corporate and commercial banking, told a meeting with MPs that, in order to comply with FSA rules, it can't allow its branch managers to make lending decisions. Pateman said the FSA would find it "unsatisfactory" if he let the "guy down in Barnstaple make the (lending) decision".

Ah well, one step forward and one step back. You have until September 20 to make your views clear to those working on the government's green paper called Financing a Private Sector Recovery.

17 November, 2010

Banks turn Cable's head

Earlier this month, the government published its response to those of us who had answered their green paper questions on financing a private-sector recovery. Sadly and worryingly, it has been hijacked by the bankers.

The original green paper was an impressive document, not least for acknowledging bank financing of SMEs cannot be relied upon: "The credit risk of the borrower is also a key element of loan pricing. Since the financial crisis, there has been a reassessment of the creditworthiness of borrowers and the expected risk of business loan defaults, leading to higher spreads on loans. To some extent, this is part of a necessary structural adjustment, following the under-pricing of risk on many business loans in previous years. SME's heavy reliance on bank credit means they are particularly vulnerable to such swings in risk appetite." [Paragraph 3.24]

The paper went on to ask 17 very pertinent questions of which, pleasingly and rightly, only two related to bank finance. More than 180 responses to these questions were received from a wide range of institutions and individuals. I particularly liked the one from Quoted Companies Alliance, which set out to argue the importance of equity finance, the need to encourage private investors, and to underline the dangers of getting into bed with our fair weather banks.

Anyway Vince Cable and co have chosen to ignore just about all of that, preferring to plump for long bouts of platitudinous verbiage about how the banks must be encouraged back into the SME space and the creation of various talking shops, all rounded off with the usual Whitehall speak that the government "will monitor developments closely".

Why such a damp squib? The answer is to be found in the following paragraph: "Seven major UK banks, working through the British Bankers' Association (BBA) to form the Business Finance Taskforce are also supplying the provision of equity finance to small and mid-sized businesses, through a new £1.5bn Business Growth Fund." And also in this one: "The government will be establishing a network of growth hubs to provide strategic advice and coaching to SMEs. The BBA is also funding and implementing a national network of business mentors."

So, down at the BBA, its clever chief executive Angela Knight has managed to turn Cable and Co's heads by spending a few bob. Why, even that other bad boy of the credit crisis, Goldman Sachs, has got in on the act, as the government response paper lovingly points out that: "Goldman Sachs is now piloting a small business support programme in Yorkshire and Humber"!

So much, then, for reforming CGT to re-energise the private investor. So much for a discussion of the role of the FSA (see my earlier article). Yes, it's back to business as usual for our big financial beasts.

5 April, 2011

Osborne should back quality not quantity

Britain's high-growth firms need significant long-term capital if they're going to make it big. So why is George Osborne still ignoring our stock markets?

George Osborne would have allowed himself a self satisfactory post-budget smile when he read a letter in the Telegraph, signed by a variety of venture capitalists and business angels, praising to the skies his Budget EIS tax breaking generosity.

Shame he is barking up the wrong tree.

The Chancellor would do better to turn to another page in the same Telegraph edition, under the headline of "Back gazelles, not start-ups". This highlights a recent report from Professor Colin Mason of the University of Strathclyde's Entrepreneurship Centre, which found that the majority of high-growth firms are not young businesses that have grown rapidly since inception but are, instead, ten years old (at least).

Said Mason: "The UK's enterprise problem is the lack of high-growth firms which go on to be companies of scale, rather than not enough start-ups. We need quality, not quantity."

These companies, of course, require significant amounts of long-term capital to finance their growth plans – and the obvious source of that should be our stock markets. Unfortunately, Osborne and Co have still not caught on to this. Why not?

Well, in my experience most politicians and venture capitalists don't recognise the importance of stock markets. This is usually because they can't be bothered to get their heads round the dynamics of what makes a flourishing stock marketplace. There are no identifiable votes in it for the politicians and the venture capitalists are usually happy either to play pass the parcel amongst themselves, or find a trade sale.

In a really excellent article, written by Anthony Hilton in the London Evening Standard on March 25 (I make no apology for quoting several parts of it), Hilton observed that the Chancellor spoke for an hour about his Budget for growth "but never once did he mention the stock market, or equity finance or the central role stock markets have in the allocation of capital throughout the economy. It just did not figure in his agenda".

Hilton went on to write: "What is really interesting – because it shows how much our society is losing the equity culture – is that no-one noticed. The death of equities is passing without comment. The primary lobbying group for the financial services industry, TheCityUK, focused on taxation and regulation but never once mentioned stock markets in its Budget reaction."

Warming to the subject, Hilton observed that "no-one seems to cotton on to the fact that you can't have healthy capitalism without healthy stock markets. We live in a world where AIM is in the doldrums."

It's hardly surprising, given that equity returns get taxed four times (as corporation tax, as CGT, as IT and as stamp duty). Osborne has left in place a tax regime which favours excessive leverage. Had he changed it, he would have rekindled enthusiasm for equities.

Sadly, we can't look to stock exchanges to promote themselves. Our largest is too busy trying to catch the wind of change on the international exchange merger scene and our institutional investors, who really should take up the cudgels, seem instead to prefer to push their counters around the FTSE 100 board.

Any other volunteers? Sir Nigel Rudd, I'm looking at you…

13 May, 2011

RBS collapse: FSA asks Mr Whitewash to investigate

The Treasury Select Committee has commissioned City grandee Sir David Walker (aka Mr Whitewash) to vet the FSA's report into the collapse of RBS. Is this a cause for celebration?

There was an understandable furore when the FSA said they would not be publishing a report into the circumstances surrounding the near failure of The Royal Bank of Scotland. The good news is the FSA has changed its mind about publishing, but the bad news is efforts to do so have become bogged down in behind-the-scenes legal squabbling.

Step forward a Knight of the Realm (and a chap called Knight). Sir David Walker and Bill Knight are charged with ensuring that the final report is fair to the bank and its former directors, and that sufficient light is shed on the FSA's role in all this.

Andrew Tyrie, chairman of the Select Committee, said: "We need to know the decisive mistakes which destroyed RBS, how they came to be, whether the FSA was asleep at the wheel, and whether we can have the confidence that they are awake now."

Leaving aside the fact that the FSA will be paying Walker and Knight to carry out their deliberations, what chance that when the report finally sees the light of day, it will have been worth the wait?

The portents are not good. Walker has spent much of his life as a fully paid-up member of the world he is being asked to take an objective view on. For many years, he was chairman and CEO of Morgan Stanley International and, as such, is no stranger to the bonus culture that may have played a large part in RBS' downfall. Even better, he was head of the FSA's forerunner

– the Securities Investment Board. A man of the establishment, if ever there was one.

Embarrassingly, in the past, some of the press dubbed him "Mr Whitewash", as many felt his previous efforts (such as formulating a code of conduct for the private equity industry and his – government sponsored – review into banks' corporate governance) had about as much effect as a windbreak in a tornado.

A perfect illustration of such is having recommended, last November, that banks should publish details of their employees' remuneration above £1m, he then managed to defend the status quo by saying in a letter to the FT : "Any attempt to require banded disclosure for UK banks in isolation would be commercially sensitive vis a vis their non-disclosing competitors elsewhere. It could also stimulate higher executive turnover, and (as a perverse unintended consequence) lead to higher remuneration as a defensive retention measure." This is nonsense. There are legions of head hunters out there who make it their business to know precisely what each of the better bank "executives" are paid.

Sadly, Cameron and Osborne fell for it. Andrew Tyrie, you've been warned!

What of Sir David's assistant in his quest for the Holy Grail in the FSA's report – one Bill Knight? There is a logic to his appointment, as he is an ex-heavyweight City lawyer and, as the FSA's opus has in part been delayed by legal wranglings, who better than a lawyer to sort them out?

Not so methinks. In situations like this, lawyers love talking to other lawyers because it is an effective way of blocking out interested onlookers as they postulate that the legal arguments are far too complicated for us mere mortals to understand.

This is often true but if, in this case, former RBS directors don't like what the FSA has to say about them, then the FSA should have the guts to say: "See you in court!" I somehow don't think those directors will fancy barristers forensically examining the evidence in public, do you?

Perhaps Knight, in his capacity as chairman of the Financial Reporting Review Panel, might instead like to examine whether RBS's auditors have a case to answer?

The Treasury Select Committee could have avoided all chances of there being a whitewash by appointing someone well away from the City's establishment. For example, a recently retired CEO of a FTSE 250 company would have fitted the bill admirably, no?

31 May, 2011

Can an affair damage your business?

The media has been recently filling up many column inches with the marital infidelities of the rich and famous. Is there a lesson for business in there?

I suppose this all kicked off (excuse the pun) with the news, under Parliamentary privilege, that no-one was permitted to so much as breathe the name Sir Fred Goodwin. This farce ended when the veil of secrecy was partially lifted to reveal that Sir Fred allegedly had a sexual dalliance with one of his senior employees.

This set me thinking about some research a fund manager colleague and I conducted a few years ago. We set out to analyse what were the root causes of our biggest investment mistakes in the companies in which we had significant shareholdings. We very quickly found out that just about all horrors fell into just two categories:

The first involved CEOs who were quite brilliant fibbers. They were so all-consumingly good at lying that not even our world-weary cynicism picked up the warning signals. The second category was much more unexpected. In several instances, the fortunes of the company had fallen off a cliff because the middle-aged CEO had decided to spice up his private life (yes, pathetically, they were all men!) by taking up with another, usually considerably younger, woman.

Could it be that playing away does damage your company?

Lord Oakeshott (himself a fund manager, so he may have had similar experiences to ours) suggested the possibility as regards Sir Fred Goodwin and requested the FSA look into it. I must say, I'm having much fun fantasising on the FSA's approach to such. The thought of some FSA drone (or perhaps the redoubtable Sir David Walker?) squaring up to Sir Fred Goodwin and saying "prove to us that dropping your trousers for Ms X had no bearing on the collapse of RBS" is just wonderful.

To be fair to Sir Fred Goodwin and other titans at the head of large organisations, such as Dominique Strauss-Kahn, our conclusions only involved small companies and if the key man in such a business takes his eye off the ball, as it were, then the company probably hasn't sufficient talented substitutes to cover for him.

Large concerns like RBS or the IMF should have much better developed infrastructure – or do they? If that large enterprise is run by a very dominant personality, surely it is possible that the whole ethos of the organisation could be at risk?

The collapse of Enron is an example. In his book Pipe Dreams, Greed, Ego and the Death of Enron, Robert Bryce quotes a Wall Street analyst's verdict on Jeff Skilling's (Enron president) sleeping around as "it addresses the character of the man. This is a guy who felt he could get away with anything. You can see it in his personal life and his business life".

Conventional wisdom (well certainly in France!) argues that your private life has no effect on your ability to do your job. In the case of politicians who are, by nature, self-obsessed, this is probably true – no matter how badly they behave, they are conditioned to just ploughing on through thick and thin.

In the case of businessmen and companies, I am not so sure.

7 July, 2011

The investor's Kryptonite: airlines, banks and textiles

A cardinal rule of personal capital preservation should be: never, ever invest in airlines, banks or textile companies. Here's why.

Airlines

Airlines are crazy businesses. Firstly you have to commit to financing equipment that is mind-blowingly expensive and requires hugely costly maintenance in order to avoid things falling out of the sky and the company covered in public opprobrium.

The equipment is frequently run by bolshie staff (eg: BA cabin crew, Virgin pilots), you have no control over the vagaries of the people who own the landing sites and, just when you think things are running smoothly, up pop volcanoes, terrorists, a few inches of snow at Heathrow, absurdly overpriced fuel, and civil wars.

I hear you say, "What about Ryanair?"

I agree it has successfully revolutionised air travel. But if you check out its share price graph, you will see the shares have more or less flatlined for the past ten years (even though it is probably the best in the business). Meanwhile, the latest stock market hopeful, Flybe, has plunged from 295p when it was listed last December to approximately 195p now. Avoid.

Banks

Where do I begin? The basic business of banking is reassuringly boring. You take money in from depositors and you lend it out, on a prudently geared basis, to customers who have the ability to repay in the agreed period. The problem is that throughout banking history there are countless examples of bankers becoming ever so bored with this (usually low-return) operation and so off they go to try their hand at new exciting things they have no experience of.

Whether it was Midland Bank buying Crocker (how apt!) Bank in the US, RBS buying ABN, lending money/dealing in shonky and inexplicable derivatives, or Bank of America buying Merrill Lynch, the list of stupidities is endless. If any of you have university-age children looking for a financial subject for their PhD, may I suggest entitling it The long and inglorious history of the banking industry?

The big problem is that those in charge don't learn from history. I see Barclays' American CEO has launched an initiative to double the bank's return on capital. That should set alarm bells ringing.

If you really can't resist the siren calls of the sector, you might like to think about Lloyds Banking Group where, encouragingly, the new CEO (Antonio Horta-Osario) said recently: "Banking is supposed to be boring in my opinion."

Personally, I'd rather avoid them all and get to sleep at night.

Textile manufacturers

About about 20 years ago, I had a sizeable investment in SR Gent, then one of the biggest suppliers of ladies' apparel to M&S. In those days, M&S made a big thing about buying

British so, when SR Gent announced it was moving a large part of its manufacturing to Sri Lanka, there was quite a kerfuffle.

Accordingly, I very quickly got to understand the first rule of textiles: no matter where you're currently manufacturing, there is always someone who can do the same cheaper elsewhere. Thus the whole thing is a global race to the bottom (as it were!). No doubt, the present holder of the textile crown, China, is beginning to experience this right now.

The rag trade can seduce: don't be lured in.

Many well-known investors like to tell you about their successes. Candidly, they would admit that much of their good fortune is down to avoiding the major duds. You know where they are!

31 October, 2011

What Josiah Wedgwood and Steve Jobs have in common

Josiah Wedgwood and Steve Jobs revolutionised their respective industries. Three centuries apart, here's what you can learn from them.

A transcript of the annual Robert Warner lecture at the Founders Company should be required reading for our captains of industry, entrepreneurs, politicians and even journalists.

Last year's tour de force was given by Will Hopper, co-author of The Puritan Gift, which argues that American business lost its way when it succumbed to the rising influence of business schools from the sixties onwards. Their seductive gospel was/is that they can train any bright graduate to walk into any senior management role in any industry and run the company far better than those poor saps who have dedicated a lifetime's experience to the same company.

As the book points out (using numerous high profile examples), these masters of business are great with statistics – but hopeless at understanding what is needed to keep delivering a quality product that people want to buy. They use much of their waking hours to figure out new ways of justifying ever higher financial reward – and too little time devoting themselves to achieving sustained growth. How true. Just look at last week's news on the average pay for a director of a FTSE 100.

This year's lecture, given by the Design Museum founder Stephen Bayley, picked up (albeit subconsciously) on the same theme.

Although he did not get off to a promising start, proclaiming that we don't make anything in Britain anymore (overly populist and simply not true), he went on to draw a very useful parallel between English potter Josiah Wedgwood and Apple's Steve Jobs.

Both men revolutionised their chosen industries because they proved, three centuries apart, that you can sell a premium priced product to the masses. Their secret was to make things of such quality, practicality and beauty that the tyranny of business school-statistics was left for dust.

Bayley's message was that if high cost-base Western economies, such as the UK and the US, want to grow their way out of recession, then their movers and shakers need to look to the likes of Wedgwood and Jobs for inspiration.

Of course, both men didn't just produce wonderful consumer goods. They were also hard-driving capitalist salesmen. Wedgwood published the world's first ever sales catalogue and Jobs had an unerring ability to mesmerise his audience and the media at product launches.

No wonder the masses flocked to buy their wares.

3 January, 2012

Optare: another British firm falls to enterprising Indians

Despite a doubling of its order book, Christmas and the New Year is not proving a happy time for British bus maker Optare as banks and the government turn their backs on it.

It's a classic example of why the "renewed push" to help finance SMEs is a load of hot air.

Granted, Optare has not enjoyed much glory as an AIM listed public company, racking up losses for several years. But the announcement just before Christmas that its board was recommending it be financed at an 80 per cent discount to its current share price by Indian-owned Ashok Leyland should raise more than a few eyebrows.

Optare was doing all the right things: it had cut its debt from over £4m to just £1.3m; it had formed an alliance with its 26 per cent Indian shareholder Ashok Leyland; and it had grown its order book from an unexciting £24m to a highly commendable £55m in the past 12 months.

Unsurprisingly, such a big leap in the order book requires additional financing and, for a company such as this, an early port of call would normally be the government's export credit insurance. But, as the company pointed out in its pre-Christmas statement: "as highlighted in previous announcements, the industry has been challenged by a lack of trade credit insurance."

So much, then, for Vince Cable and his favourite ex banker Lord Green at UK Trade & Investment.

The next port of call is, of course, Optare's bankers. But the company warned in September that it was still in "constructive discussions" with them so, with the help of Ashok's financial muscle, facilities were extended by just three months.

As we now know, the bankers took fright at increasing credit lines to a required £12m despite the vastly improved order book, a strong and productive industry shareholder and a company that had made all the right debt management moves so far. Certainly no sign of our banks' "renewed enthusiasm" for SME lending.

What of Optare's British shareholders? Two of its largest are the venerable old names of Legal & General and M&G/ Prudential, who certainly have the financial firepower. Sadly, as Optare's entire market capitalisation was just £6m, is anyone in those august institutions going to stick their necks out to the tune of £12m? I think not.

So, with no help coming from any of its other stakeholders, Ashok Leyland quite understandably went in for the kill. In return for providing the credit line, it is taking its shareholding up to 75 per cent by injecting £4m at an 80 per cent discount to the existing share price. This must be particularly eye-watering for Optare's finance director Peter Phillips, who was cheerfully buying stock at ten times this price just six months ago.

Post-Christmas, there was one last little twist to this tale when up popped a competitor Alexander Dennis (a group backed by Scottish millionaire Sir Brian Souter) who said it was considering making an offer for the company. Unsurprisingly, Ashok told Dennis to sling its hook as their shareholding was not for sale "to anyone at any price" and Dennis has duly backed off. Shareholder approval is set for this Friday (January 6) and, short of a Damascene conversion by its current British shareholders on the day, we will just have to watch another British company fall to enterprising Indians.

21 February, 2012

Has the FT given up on British businesses?

"No FT, no comment" was the simple but effective slogan of our best known British financial journal a while back. Is this still the case?

Sadly not any more if you are a home-grown business.

Last week I selected, at random, two days' worth of the "Companies and Markets" section of the FT and, yes, it is actually devoted to reporting on companies and market events. Having parted with a not-to-be-sniffed-at £2.50 per paper, you could be forgiven for expecting some news and thoughts on a broad range of UK companies and yes, each day, seven pages are available to be filled with such. But what do we find there?

My £5 worth covered 17 articles on US companies, 13 on Continental European, 10 on the rest of the world and just 7 on ours. Yes there were another 5 on FTSE 100 constituents but, as they tend to have operations all over the world, they hardly fit into domestic coverage.

Why would most of us want to read articles entitled "Orange to offer Facebook in Africa" or "Cisco to appeal against Skype takeover clearance" or "Danone cuts sales and margin targets"?

President Sarkozy might be relieved to read "L'Oreal ready for the next generation" and mildly interested in "France Telecom hits out at rival" but why should you or I care?

Meanwhile "ThyssenKrupp blames net loss on weaker demand" and "Hamburg to take biggest stake in Hapag-Lloyd" is hardly going to rouse the interest of those on the 07.43 to Cannon street, or indeed heading to work anywhere else in Britain, is it?

Just a very few years ago, the "Pink 'Un" not only used to report on a considerable number of our companies every day but many of these were also accompanied by a comment section, which analysed and gave an opinion on the business in question. No chance of that now.

And it doesn't get any better when it comes to writing about our circa 1,700 companies in the small-cap sectors. Just two were mentioned in the London stock market report section over my two-day sample.

What has gone wrong?

The answer is that the paper has become obsessed with painting itself as an international beastie.

The last nail in the coffin for reporting on our companies was when the excellent David Blackwell (twice winner of the AIM analyst of the Year Award) decided to plump for early retirement at the end of last year. Result? The latest circulation figures show they are selling a pathetic 70,478 papers in the UK and Ireland and just 220,027 for all their efforts everywhere else.

When you try to be all things to all those interested in finance and commerce, you end up appealing to no-one.

There are a few positives that its tiny subscriber base can still look to, namely three first-class columnists in Gillian Tett (general banking and international finance), Wolfgang Munchau (comment on the absurdities of Euroland) and Lucy Kellaway (excellent at sending up corporate speak). But that's about it.

The FT used to be required reading for all those working in the London corporate markets and for most SME business leaders. Not anymore.

At a time when everyone from government ministers to the CBI, IOD, the ICAEW, and even bankers are looking to encourage British businesses, the fact that the most established home-grown journal of the past 120 years has almost become an irrelevance here is absurd.

Can someone shake it up before it gives up on us altogether?

15 March, 2012

Banks mis-selling to SMEs: will the FSA act?

The most recent edition of the Sunday Telegraph looks to have unearthed a particularly nasty form of mis-selling to SMEs. Will the FSA act or will it reconfirm some commentators' label as the "Fundamentally Supine Authority"?

The Sunday Telegraph believes that our fine upstanding high street banks have sold "unnecessarily complex and inappropriate interest rate swaps to small business customers".

An extraordinary swathe of customers ranging from fish and chip shops to B&Bs, boarding kennels, farmers, one-man-band retailers, solicitors, as well as slightly bigger enterprises such as engineering companies and care homes have been signed up to these complex instruments.

The common complaint here is that loans – especially those taken out between 2005 and 2007 by these unfortunate enterprises – were often accompanied by an invitation to shield the borrower from interest rate rises by taking out interest rate swaps. What these borrowers didn't appreciate was that if interest rates fell very significantly, which of course they have done from 2008 onwards, the costs of servicing the loan went up very considerably.

The experience of Paul Adcock, owner of a small electronic retailing family business that has banked with Barclays for 100 years is particularly illuminating. In 2007, according to Mr Adcock and the Sunday Telegraph, having been pursued by a young Barclays relationship manager for twelve months ("he would just not let go") he signed up to what is known in the banking world as an asymmetric leverage collar interest rate swap.

Mr Adcock told the Telegraph that because he had a very large (for him) £970,000 loan with Barclays, he felt it was best to do as they suggested as at least it would protect him from rising rates. He admits he didn't really understand what would happen if interest rates fell. Hardly surprising, as it took two days for a former senior derivatives banker to work out what Barclays had done to Mr Adcock – "normally it takes me half an hour, but this was a real bastard of a thing".

Unsurprisingly, the derivatives specialist concluded that this instrument was completely inappropriate for Adcocks of Watton. You would hope, after all that, that Barclay's would say "alright it's a fair cop," wouldn't you? No chance.

In a statement, Barclays said it is "satisfied that it provides sufficient information to enable a client to make an informed commercial decision about the product it offers". In other words: tough luck, not our fault if you don't understand the small print.

As James Dean, the MD of Legal Plus, which is handling dozens of cases on behalf of small firms, points out, "I have seen hundreds of people who are desperately caught up by this. They are not sharp-suited companies. They are ordinary businesses."

Where is the FSA in all this mess? Well I was particularly heartened to read today that their new MD, Martin Wheatley, warned that the UK financial services industry "destroys trust" by aggressively selling complex, expensive products to retail investors and must put customers' interests first.

While these are not retail customers, surely even the FSA understands there is a big case to answer? Ah well, you see, "it is a complicated issue and that is all we want to say at this time", said an FSA spokesman to the Telegraph.

What the Fundamentally Supine Authority means is that interest rate swaps aren't regulated, so can they really be bothered to get into yet another mis-selling struggle with our well-resourced-and-subsidised-by-us banking industry?

Mercifully, there is one ray of light. The Treasury, which as I've said before is the only institution that the "politicians" at the FSA pay scrupulous attention to, are saying "we will review this issue closely, alongside the FSA and the Financial Ombudsmen Service, to ensure that businesses have been sold those products in a clear and understandable way"

Get to it FSA. In the meantime, the high street banks' protestations that they are doing all they can to help Britain's small businesses look ever more shallow by the day.

19 March, 2012

Banks mis-selling to SMEs: an update

Following on from the Telegraph's exposé about banks mis-selling to SMEs, the FSA has agreed to listen to business owners. Hurrah?

A short update to my piece last week about banks mis-selling to SMEs:

The latest edition of The Sunday Telegraph says it has been inundated with complaints from business owners over the sale of interest rate swaps.

The FSA is now saying "if there's anyone who would like us to look at evidence they would be welcome to contact us", which is a bit of a change from "it is a complicated issue and that is all we want to say at this time".

A chap called Jeremy Roe has set up a website called Bully-Banks.co.uk to help affected small businesses co-ordinate their response. If you feel you have not understood your interest rate swop then that may well be worth a visit.

2 April, 2012

Q: What do the UK Treasury and call centres have in common?

A: They both have similar levels of staff turnover. No wonder we can't get any sense out of the Treasury when it comes to policies on SMEs, pasties or anything else.

A rare and courageous review commissioned by Sir Nicholas Macpherson, permanent secretary to the Treasury, found that staff turnover in the UK Treasury was three times higher than anywhere else in the civil service.

"Such high turnover is more commonly found in semi-skilled parts of the service sector such as call centres or hospitality," said the review's author Sharon White, in a put-down worthy of Maggie Smith in Downton Abbey.

Even worse, more than half its policy advisers have been in the role for less than three years. As one Treasury official told White: "There has been a lot of turnover and it is difficult to find out what has been happening in relevant policy areas."

This frightening lack of experience explains a lot when it comes to figuring out why SMEs find most of Whitehall's attempts to understand their world haphazard and amateurish.

Take, for example, the Breedon Review on access to finance for SMEs, which was designed to help Osborne and Co understand their policy options.

Not a single entrepreneur or small-business owner made it onto the taskforce. Indeed the three taskforce members who showed up at the review's launch at the ICAEW consisted of Tim Breedon, CEO of Legal and General (main business experience: creation of passive fund index investing); Julian Franks, a professor at London Business School; and Charles Roxburgh, a director of McKinsey.

Moreover, Breedon admitted at the launch that they had only been commissioned to look at debt finance and to ignore equity finance, thus making the whole thing very lopsided and incomplete.

Even the useful finance initiatives that Osborne announced in November's Autumn Statement had started to fall apart by the time he got on his feet in last month's Budget.

Take the EIS and VCT schemes. Instead of raising the annual investment limit for qualifying companies from £2m to £10m, it was set at £5m. Brussels has reminded the bright young things at the Treasury (average age: 32, according to the redoubtable Sharon White) that any more would break State Aid rules.

Even the £5m has yet to be approved by the Eurocrats so, for now, we are back down to the old £2m limit!

This is simple incompetence. Either the Treasury should possess sufficient financial acumen to be able to put Brussels back in its box or it should make sure it doesn't serve up a policy it can't deliver.

Sharon White recommends that the Treasury "place greater emphasis on experience, expertise and people management in its promotion and reward policies". Until it does, the ability of big business to elbow out SME interests by dazzling young civil servants and ministers will continue unabated.

Evidence of that was seen in a letter to the FT last week where the writer pointed out that the PM's Business Advisory Council includes just one token entrepreneur (Sir James Dyson) among a plethora of "big company" men and women. To quote from the letter: "The truth is that SMEs tend not to employ lobbyists, make generous donations to political parties or offer sinecures to retired politicians and mandarins. As a result, the public policy needs of these entrepreneurial businesses making their way in the world will always be subordinated to the interests of those already seated at the top table."

Until the Treasury starts recruiting more staff who actually have experience of what they are talking about, SMEs and their supporters will continue to whistle Dixie.

11 June, 2012

The return of the dividend?

Why do those without business experience decide over our companies, asks The City Grump. An expensive new SME enterprise research centre is far from what we need.

The following "highlights" from a press release this week must surely make those of us at the sharp end of smaller company finance run from the room screaming obscenities and rush into the nearest pub for solace:

"A partnership to create a new independent £2.9m enterprise research centre that will help drive Government policy for SMEs in the UK has been announced. The Enterprise Research Centre will help develop a greater understanding of the factors affecting business investment, performance and growth. It is a joint collaboration between the Department for Business, Innovation and Skills (BIS), the British Bankers Association (BBA), the Economic and Social Research Council (ESRC) and the Technology Strategy Board. The call for proposals to form the centre opens today, and will close on 4 September 2012. Applications are welcomed from academic institutions across the UK with relevant expertise. It is expected that the successful bidder will be announced in the autumn.

Angela Knight, chief executive of the British Bankers' Association, said: "Information is key to delivering investment and for targeting help and support where it is needed most. The British Bankers' Association and major UK banks are delighted to support the Enterprise Research Centre, an initiative which will see research focusing on small and medium sized enterprises. We believe the insight we gain will help inform policy, provide a focal point for research, bring key knowledge together in one place and help banks better serve their businesses customers. We also hope the research will help policy makers, business organisations and investors to work together to further develop initiatives that support enterprise and the UK growth agenda."

So, we have £2.9m of our money wasted on a talking shop between our lame duck banks, who haven't got the money. If you want further on this read Liam Halligan's Sunday Telegraph article about the zombie bank malaise, bureaucrats indulging in yet another Quango and a bunch of academics who have no business experience whatsoever.

What do George and Vince have against talking to those who have actually spent a lifetime running SMEs and/or helping them raise capital? As a colleague of mine despairingly put it, "we could collectively tell them the answer for the price of a good dinner". George Osborne could even avoid that expense if he cared to ease on round to the ancestral home and ask his father for views and suggestions. He at least has long experience of running an SME (Osborne & Little).

Of course I do not expect the Government to take heed of the City Grump, do another of its celebrated U-turns and can this Quango in the making, but perhaps they and the readers of this column might like to think about the following:

Xavier Rolet, the CEO of the London Stock Exchange, said this week, "Equity was invented here but today it's become effectively an almost dead asset class."

How true. Why so and what can be done? This happened due to a deadly combination of ever increasing regulation over equity investing (as opposed to other forms of capital with little or no regulation) and an insistence that the income stream from government bonds is the most reliable way of meeting the requirements of policyholders, by the actuarial advisors to our pension funds and insurance companies

When I started in investment management back in the 1970s, the prevailing view was that the way to value a company was through its dividend stream. In other words, companies that paid dividends were more valuable than those that didn't. Companies that paid a rising dividend every year where the most valuable of the lot. Thanks to the actuarial advice outlined above, that approach went out the window years ago.

Now, so-called 'growth companies', especially SMEs, have been able to hide behind the "we don't need to pay out dividends to our investors because we can better employ it in our business" tack. Imagine trying to suggest that as a reason to your banker, for why you shouldn't pay any interest on that loan.

I sense the pendulum is beginning to swing back. UK government bonds now provide the lowest income since records began in the 18th Century. Until recently the US technology sector paid negligible dividends. Goldman Sachs predicts dividends of US technology companies will double again in the next two years, making the sector the biggest contributor in S&P Index. Investors are desperate for income and will look increasingly favourably on any companies they think can provide them such.

I know this defies conventional wisdom, but if you are running a small or mid-sized company and are beginning to despair of attracting investment, then think hard about how your business can generate a dividend stream. You'll find investors beating a path to your door and then the £2.9m Enterprise Research Centre can shut up its talking shop.

31 August, 2012

Now would be a good time to reset both our rules and our values (Part II)

Investor expectations are pushing companies to the edge of their competencies. Surely there's a better way to connect businesses and those who run their money? The answer is in James Featherby's Of Markets and Men.

In part II of the City Grump's series of extracts from the excellent "Of Markets and Men", its author, James Featherby, draws out the disconnect between money managers and those who give them the money: you and me.

Asset managers are losing themselves in a sea of speculation and hypothetical returns. In turn, many large companies are taking ever greater operational risks in pursuit of high performance. Featherby suggests an intriguing new way we can re-engage with those who run our money and with the companies they invest in. Read on!

"Speculative trading is problematic partly because there is no sense of responsibility for any underlying business or the economy as a whole, and if you are not responsible you are unlikely to care. Similarly, claims based trading, hedging arrangements that in return for a price allow us to make financial claims on others that do not vary depending on their future profitability, has produced a financial climate in which too many are uninterested in the welfare of society or the business that produces those profits. Together, speculative and claims-based trading have begun to be destructive to the process of efficient capital allocation. The market was not designed to be used for these purposes on this scale.

"The decision making process of many asset managers, including pension funds and insurance companies, is heavily influenced by statisticians and actuaries with little expertise in the business of business. They have the prime seats at the table, and they steer the conversation towards sectoral asset allocation and hypothetical returns, not individual investments and specific implications. We should not quickly forget that the economic theories of rational expectations and efficient markets failed to predict or prevent the financial crisis or the massive loss of share values that followed. And it is now clear that there are no risk free assets. Models that pretend otherwise are just as likely to misallocate capital as good old fashioned business judgement.

"Companies are also increasingly operating at the edge of their competencies as a result of competitive pressures and investor expectations. This seems to have been the case with BP's Deepwater Horizon, but it is also the case amongst banks, insurance companies and financial investors trading in securities they may not fully understand.

"The investment in research and development of new technology for products and services including financial ones is increasingly out of balance with the investment devoted to risk identification, prevention and remediation. There was, for example, significant underinvestment by the banks in in the infrastructure necessary to understand and manage the sub-prime products they held on their balance sheets. And when a large player in a market makes a competency mistake the risk to society is increased because the consequences of that mistake tend to reverberate louder and further.

"In the name of efficiency, there has also been a significant change in recent years in the trade-off between business stability and financial efficiency. Many businesses now carry minimal stock, outsource vital functions to third parties they cannot control, rely on suppliers without giving them support, and leverage their operations with significant debt. In other words, businesses are taking greater risks with less inbuilt operational resilience; and others are frequently feeling the consequences when the business stumbles or falls. The consequences are amplified when the business is big.

"Scale also reduces the resilience of society in another respect. Companies tend to have command and control mentalities. This means that, even after a period of reflection, they tend to take one-way bets with their strategic decisions. Their inclination is to develop a single house view, and then follow it closely. And given the human tendency to believe and follow conventional wisdom this makes them, and therefore the rest of the economy, less resilient to life's uncertainties.

"Diversification by mega-businesses, including full service banks, does not avoid systemic risk if all those businesses are diversifying in the same way. Diversity of business model, a different concept entirely, is more beneficial to society. Complex and diverse is more resilient than complex and similar.

"Modern investment has mostly become a mathematical exercise where the investor seeks to maximise its financial return commensurate with risk. It is largely uninterested in where or how the money is invested. We do not want farms that produce at the edge of the envelope: no matter what the season or the weather producing food to their maximum capacity and without regard to what that means in terms of soil fatigue, animal welfare, bio diversity, disease resilience, and frankly sheer enjoyment of the countryside.

"In the end a farm run at the edge of the envelope will die of exhaustion. We do not want that in farming. We should not want that in investing. Bi-productive investment, by contrast, intentionally seeks to be productive twice – for the investor at one end of the investment chain, and for the company and its other stakeholders at the other end.

"The heroes (of investment management) might no longer be mathematicians and nuclear physicists who can construct ever more intricate trading strategies. They might become social and environmental experts who can best advise how to channel private sector finance for the benefit of both society and investors.

"Significantly, moving towards bi-productive investment would re-connect investors with their investments, and perhaps this would be the most profound change of all. Our current investment arrangements mean that we are disconnected from where the money is invested. Few of us could name the top 10 companies in which our savings and pensions are invested. With that level of knowledge it is no wonder that we do not care what the companies do with our money, how they treat their staff, or how they handle environmental challenges. With bi-productive investment care and interest stand at the beginning of the investment process and are not left as possible by-products that are in practice usually forgotten.

"Man was born free but everywhere his investment advisor has tethered him to anxiety. As many have remarked, our attitude to investing has historically been dominated by fear and greed, to one degree or another. Our isolationist, reductionist, utilitarian and controlling values make us poor investors. We do not want to look a fool either by doing worse than everyone else or by missing out on opportunities that might have made us richer.

"What if we decided instead that life was better when it was more of an adventure? Would we be more philosophical about any temporary setbacks in financial return, and more delighted by any unexpected financial successes? Would our savings and investments turn from being a hoard to be protected into a source of pleasure and surprise?

"Connecting investors with the purposes to which their capital is put would radically reform notions of stewardship. We would see an investment environment develop that was far less short-term as investors came to appreciate that time is needed to produce and sustain financial, social and environmental benefits.

"In turn, this would transform the objectives and incentives of company directors and business managers, who would no longer find themselves under pressure to manage for short-term financial outcomes rather than invest in research, development and productivity.

"Businesses would develop a clearer sense of purpose, and a greater understanding of their social usefulness and this would lead to improved staff moral and engagement businesses would be clearer at board level about corporate objectives and about communicating those objectives internally and externally.

"We may need a new metaphor for business and its connection with the society of which it forms a part, including other businesses. The invisible hand is past its sell-by date, not least because the picture it paints is too individualistic. Business as jazz may be a more useful metaphor: an orchestra of different players, both within and alongside each business, each weaving their harmonies into the rhythm of the whole: every participant aware of and responding to the contribution of others; each instrument making its own unique contribution. One song. Many voices."

23 October, 2012

Are we wasting our time on small business entrepreneurs?

James Harris ends his article for Real Business with, "The plight of the small business entrepreneur is a narrative that has proved all too seductive. Whether there is any truth to it is another matter."

In essence, he is asking the question, "Are we all wasting time worrying about ways we can get capital into our small companies?" No, we are not.

Most of James' article concentrates on the futility of coercing banks into funding small companies. Absolutely right – but in so doing he breezes past what the old 3i achieved and suggests that equity finance is for the birds. "What companies need is working capital, which is hard to fund with equity – entrepreneurs think it's too expensive." And anyway, why bother fussing about all this as, "there is no evidence to suggest that high levels of small business financing leads to dynamic economies."

Oh dear! Those of us who are old enough to have experienced the vintage years of 3i at first hand will remember that it spawned literally hundreds of small companies up and down the land, many of which went onto traded equity markets and raised further capital from other investors to expand their businesses. An excellent example of wealth generation for our country.

And since when was it not a good idea to raise equity to fund working capital? The very nature of a growing small company is that it consumes working capital. Most outward looking entrepreneurs of course know this and understand that equity capital is the safe, non-recourse way of ensuring their businesses are built on solid foundations.

The problem is that our small-cap equity markets are suffering from regulatory attack and a government that has forgotten what a powerful force for growth they can be. So the latest absurdity (obscenity?) from the FSA is that they are now (FSA Consultation Paper CP12/19) trying to prevent the public from investing in small companies through the tried and tested medium of fully listed Venture Capital Trusts, many of which have been at the heart of small company funding for the last 15 years.

A bit over a decade ago, the ability of small companies to raise capital on our premier market, AIM, was enormously helped by limiting CGT to just ten per cent. This provided a very straightforward virtuous circle, namely low CGT encouraged investors to trade small companies, which in turn led to greater liquidity, which in turn led to more IPOs and secondary fund raisings, which in turn led to more employment, which in turn led to more taxes being generated – KISS (Keep It Simple Stupid) at its most obvious! Foolishly, those low tax days are long gone and from a CGT perspective you might as well invest in some FTSE 100 megalith.

When all is said and done, are those small entrepreneurs at the heart of a dynamic economy? Well, according to a report in the Financial Times this month large businesses' share of employment in the UK dropped from 45 to 40 per cent between 2000 and 2011, showing that multinationals are more likely to shed jobs than create them. Let's raise a glass to our brilliant small businesses!

14 November, 2012

What's happened to your pension?

Last week I received a nasty shock when I realised that the new holders of those venerable posts of the Archbishop of Canterbury and the Lord Mayor of London are younger than me. This makes me feel very old indeed and, naturally, my thoughts turned the looming trappings of the "third age".

One reward to look forward to in a developed economy such as ours is, of course, a worthwhile pension. Not anymore, thanks to the incessant meddling of the Bank of England and the seemingly all-powerful FSA.

Another shock to my general sense of wellbeing last week

was to be told that for the first time since the 1950s UK pension funds hold more bonds than equities (43.2 per cent compared with 38.5 per cent).

Why is this?

In two words: quantitative easing.

For years now, the Bank of England has been artificially lowering bond yields by buying up vast quantities of gilts (they now own a staggering one-third of all UK gilts in existence).

In other words, they have cornered the market – a practice, by the way, that if you or I had tried, we would be banged up by our friends at the FSA.

Why does this affect your pension?

It has been some time that the Pensions Regulator and the FSA have insisted that bonds are relatively risk free (compared to equity) investments and therefore must feature, big time, in pension funds. But the BoE's manipulation of falling yields means that ever more bonds have to be purchased by your harassed pension fund manager in an effort to match the actuarial requirements of your pension. This is madness.

The BoE and the FSA have become the Scylla and Charybdis of your pension as, like those mythical Greek sea monsters, they try to suck your fund managers into the vortex of doom.

Indeed the FSA has just announced to the industry that they must lower their illustrative rates of return from seven per cent to five per cent per annum. An FSA spokesman said the regulator wants to stop companies giving savers the "false impression that they are likely to get huge returns".

The FSA said that a central rate of seven per cent is "inappropriate" given the current economic uncertainty: "We think that people who are making a long term investment decision deserve to have a pretty good indication of what they are likely to get back."

Perfect! In a few short sentences the FSA has demonstrated why it should have nothing to do with your pension.

Firstly, they underline the fact that current returns are disappointing due to their forcing us into "risk free" bonds and secondly they make the cardinal schoolchild error of projecting today's investment climate into the long term decision making process.

We have gone full circle back to the 1950s when George Ross Goobey made his seminal speech pointing out that pension funds should hold more equities as it was only equity investments that are capable of providing a rising income stream through growing dividends, thus lowering pension funds' actuarial liabilities.

Companies are in business to grow over the long term. When they grow they are capable of paying out growing dividends. Pension fund managers should be set free to take this common sense approach to investing your pension pot. Otherwise they will remain trapped in their Kafkaesque bureaucratic nightmare and your pension will continue its disappearing act.

21 March, 2014

People should be trusted to make their own financial decisions

The consequences of George Osborne empowering us to do as we wish with our pension pots are truly massive. Not least for investment in SMEs.

As the editorial in the Telegraph pointed out: "trusting pensioners with their own money is such a novel idea in modern politics that many MPs and commentators were unsure how to respond.

On the Left, in particular, the view that government knows best what should be done with citizens' money is so ingrained that there has been instinctive suspicion of the very idea that we might be allowed to decide for ourselves".

The Financial Conduct Authority has always taken its political cue from the nanny knows best culture so Osborne's radical move to let you and I make our own financial decisions will come as a huge shock to them.

And here's the revolution, of which some of the consequences should at long last enable our small companies to communicate directly to the UK's adult population about making an investment in them.

Since the dawn of financial regulation, unsurprisingly the FCA and its predecessors have always obsessed about the possibility that a granny somewhere may put her life savings into an "inappropriate investment" (their terminology) and when it goes wrong our politicians will very publicly blame them for allowing her to do such.

Now Westminster has set free grannies and granddads everywhere to do as they wish. So, with one Budgetary stroke, the vast panoply of regulation that is designed to ascertain whether it is "appropriate" you and I take an investment in, for example a small company through a crowdfunding platform or one listed on AIM, comes crashing to the ground.

Allow me to illustrate. At present if you go to a private client investment management organisation such as Brewin Dolphin or Charles Stanley or an Independent financial adviser, and say to them I would like you to manage my spare cash and I want you to put it into small companies (such as those traded on AIM), the manager/advisor is compelled by the FCA to ascertain whether they believe you are in a position to understand the risk of small company investing.

Sadly the inevitable consequence is that nine out of ten managers/advisors cannot be bothered with the regulatory aggravation and so will turn your business away.

Concerning equity crowdfunding, because this is a new entrant the FCA has decided to make up new rules, including the absurd rule that no adult coming into crowdfunding on his own accord will be allowed to invest no more than 10 per cent of his net assets in non-readily realisable assets (whatever they are and not defined by the FCA). The crowdfunders "must assess the appropriateness of clients wanting to invest without professional advisors" said an FCA spokesman.

The inevitable consequence of Osborne's revolutionary move is that the FCA is now badly out of step with its political masters and the logical conclusion is that the FCA's barriers to investing in small companies should be swept away. No longer need they obsess about granny.

It won't have had time to yet but I look forward to the Treasury telling the financial regulator just that. But just in case there is any backsliding do write to your local MP and bring them up to speed.

12 December 2014

Is the Financial Misconduct Authority a regulator unfit for purpose?

Clifford Chance partner Simon Davis' 225-page study of the FCA induced major falls in Insurance Companies' share prices and the ensuing false market, on the 28th March this year, is a devastating insight into how unfit for purpose our financial regulator is and why this is so.

Davis reminds the reader that the FCA's overarching strategic objective is to ensure that the relevant markets function well. Many of us who have had dealings with the FCA and its predecessor have always known that the culture has fostered a dangerous ignorance of the functioning mechanisms of what it is charged to regulate. This was the case with our equity markets last March. In the same way a traffic warden knows how to hand out a parking ticket but doesn't know how the car he is ticketing works, Davis found swathes of the FCA ignorant as to what constitutes price sensitive information.

In their obsession with fulfilling supremo Martin Wheatley's edict that the use of the media is "a necessary tool of regulation" (para 8.4 of the Report), FCA employees forgot to consider market sensitive information when they briefed Daily Telegraph reporter Dan Hyde on what they were planning to examine in their upcoming Insurance Company Review. Shockingly this is not at all surprising as Davis discovered.

"There is no dedicated section in the Employee Handbook

relating to price-sensitive information specifically, nor does the Employee Handbook contain any detailed guidelines as to either the identification of price-sensitive information by FCA employees or procedures for the control and release of such information once identified" (7.22). In other words, it doesn't form part of employee culture.

On the other hand, no doubt senior FCA employees are well aware of Wheatley's observation that "we deliver regulation over products that cater for every single person in this country. So if 50m people want to know what's going on they won't get it from reading our website they will get it from stories that exist in the media. So my answer is the media is a very powerful tool, of course it is, and that is what we use" (8.4).

Extraordinary! Simon Davis also unearthed that in their internal paper on whether to release to the media an intention to produce a thematic review "under the heading 'Are There Any Risks Involved?' A key reputational risk identified in announcing thematic reviews early is that the FCA could not reach the deadlines to which it had committed. The paper contains a series of boxes which were completed dealing with, for example, competition, equality and diversity implications of the proposal. There was no box required to be completed addressing the implication of the release of price sensitive information. Nor was the risk of disseminating price-sensitive information otherwise addressed" (8.27,8.28).

So what happens when the Telegraph breaks the story it has been briefed on and prices of London Stock Exchange listed Insurance Companies start crashing? The reactions and actions of very senior FCA employees is painfully revealing of just what is wrong with our regulator.

Simon Davis reports that:

At 9am Clive Adamson, director of Supervision, having been rung by a furious insurance company executive, realised that price sensitive information had been given to the Telegraph and ordered his team to make a "public" retraction. His team took that to mean that they should brief other media organisations rather than issue a retraction through the Stock Exchange's announcement system. Share prices continued to fall.

At 9.40am Mr Teasdale, the head of the UK Listing Authority (part of the FCA), told Mr Spens, head of market monitoring (one of the few real practitioners at the regulator as he had previously been head of proprietary trading at Citygroup) that the FCA may have briefed the Telegraph with price sensitive information.

At 10am, Spens informed Mr Lawton, director of the markets division of the situation. A few minutes later Lawton discussed the situation with Ms McMillan, director of communications as to whether they should make a Stock Exchange Announcement (an RNS). To quote Simon Davis' report: "Lawton [stated] that the pro of an RNS was that the FCA would then have followed best practice in relation to price-sensitive information." However, the information was now publicly available and was being covered widely by the news media. The con, Lawton identified, was that announcing via an RNS would cause the market to question why the FCA was distributing the information via an RNS now, drawing attention to how the information had been disseminated by the FCA, and he was concerned about the FCA's reputation (paras 15.91 and 15.92).

At 10.25 Spens met with Martin Wheatley's executive assistant "and said he was angry because the FCA might have breached its own guidance and might have committed market abuse". (15.120) The executive assistant relayed Spens' concerns to Wheatley but said that Lawton felt a statement was not needed.

At 11am Wheatley was interviewed by the BBC and he said only after that, at 11.30, he appreciated that the FCA had a serious issue, that no-one appeared to have taken charge and that subject to confirmation from the UK Listing Authority the FCA needed to issue a statement as quickly as possible (para 15.138).

Instead of calling senior staff together in one room in order to speedily hammer out the required statement, Wheatley made the mistake of allowing them to spend the next two hours drifting back and forth with emails and individual discussions. One of the more revealing ones was from Spens to Wheatley's executive assistant: "I appreciate others may not get this point but our biggest mistake is if the FT pick up the 'Market Watch Issue No. 37' (This was a bulletin issued to member firms about how to proceed with price-sensitive information). I've read what we sent to the Telegraph and it is not as bad as I first imagined. We can probably spin that it was not price-sensitive and that the Telegraph spun it. I am stretching though." (15.176)

At 1.40 pm the chairman of the FCA, Mr Griffiths-Jones spoke to John Kingman, the second permanent secretary of the Treasury. Kingman told him that HM Treasury were concerned that the FCA might have moved markets and insurance companies had been calling HM Treasury all morning, saying they were getting mixed messages from investors and FCA junior staff. Kingman questioned why the FCA was pre-briefing at all and said that if a listed company had acted in the same way, there would be serious consequences. Kingman advised strongly that the FCA make an announcement that day. Kingman also gave his view that the FCA should mount an independent enquiry into the events. (paras 15.192 and 15.193).

At 2.27, some six hours after the Stock Exchange had started trading, the FCA released an Exchange Announcement clarifying its position. Share prices of the affected companies immediately improved.

The Davis Report may have cost north of £3m but it carefully points to the inescapable fact that the FCA is culturally incapable of fulfilling its statutory requirement of ensuring financial markets function well. It has become fixated with the political pastimes of media and image and has, in doing so, forgotten the difference between what is right and what is wrong. Those whom it regulates and our country deserve much, much better.

The following must happen now:

- Martin Wheatley, the architect of the culture of using the media as a regulatory tool must be replaced;
- Adamson and McMillan left the FCA this week. They should be joined by Lawton and many others whose activities Davis described;
- There needs to be a root and branch re-training of FCA employees, so that they thoroughly understand their public responsibilities; and
- All those investors who sold stock in insurance companies between the opening of the London Stock Exchange on March 28th 2014 and 2.27 that day, must be recompensed for their losses by the FCA.

20 July 2015

FCA CEO Martin Wheatley's removal could signal a new era in terms of investment

When we look back in five years' time, the ejection of the FCA's CEO, Martin Wheatley, may have proven to be the catalyst for the capital advancement of British companies.

Why? Because the political wind is beginning to blow favourably towards those who realise our regulator needs to move away from discouraging you and I to invest as we please.

Chancellor George Osborne, who is clearly behind Wheatley's dismissal , said "a different leadership" is needed to take the FCA forward. In other words the betting has to be Wheatley's successor won't be as outdated and wrongheaded as he was.

Earlier this year I gave a speech, controversial at the time, entitled "Our regulator doesn't understand investment". I set out to identify the heart of the problem. Little did I know then that my views seem to be heading into the mainstream! Here is the keynote from it:

"Many of us realised a long time ago that financial regulation has little to do with regulation and everything to do with politics. The FCA is obsessed by the thought that one day a little old lady may lose her life savings of £5,000 in an investment, complains to her MP who then stands up in parliament and wants to know what the regulator is doing about it. The whole culture is driven by this fear and that doesn't lead to a healthy understanding of what investment is."

An excellent book by the recent CEO of Berenberg Bank Andrew McNally called "Debtonator" was published the other day. In it he draws attention to the inevitable consequences of this overarching culture of fear and protection. He said: "Regulators have become obsessed with protection: pensions need protecting, consumers need protecting and savers need protecting. On one level they are right – protection from poor or fraudulent business practices is essential – but protection has turned to denial of equity ownership not just in the regulators' approach to pension funds but in the setting of society's approach to risk.

"We have to ask ourselves if we've sleepwalked into a regulatory environment in which we discourage too many not to claim a stake in the rewards of economic progress itself. As to what they call 'risk assets', a scary way to describe equity these, are deemed unsuitable for everyone apart from those who can tolerate 'the risk'.

"In other words that fear of the little old lady beating the regulator about the head has blinded the FCA to what investment is all about. Hence our pension funds are ordered to fill their portfolios with 'safe' government bonds as compared to 'risky' equities (despite the fact that over any long term period you care to measure in the last 100 years equities naturally outperform bonds), retail investors are discouraged from investing other than through fund managers who are forced to carry out ludicrous 'suitability' tests, and something new like the democratisation of investment through crowdfunding is viewed with fear and loathing by our regulators, sitting out there in Canary Wharf.

"In summary I believe our regulator has essentially become little more than an over zealous traffic warden. A traffic warden knows how to put a parking ticket on a car but he is not obliged to understand how that car works. Indeed the mechanics and motive force of investment are, very sadly, beyond our regulator's understanding for now."

The FCA's new CEO has a massive job to do to change the culture and understanding of North Colonnade. The size of the task was laid bare by the admirable Simon Davis who produced a forensic but highly readable report into the regulator's breathtakingly inept handling of price sensitive information concerning quoted insurance companies in March 2014. A summary of this can be found in my City Grump article.

Not only will he/she have to retrain the staff but also politicians, and indeed journalists, will need to be persuaded to take a more mature and far-sighted attitude to our citizens experiencing the natural ups and downs of personal investment. The omens are reasonable, as exemplified by the courageous decision of the previous Government in setting the public free to choose what they do with their pension pots, but there is a long road to travel yet.

For just as the Spanish Inquisition attempted to hold back the development of religious progress, Wheatley's FCA set out to prevent all of us from making our own investment decisions, with disastrous consequences for the ability of our next generation of companies to attract that investment. For all our futures we must pray that his passing ends this current destructively nihilistic regulatory era.

4 September 2015

Mission Impossible: Bank of England's Andy Haldane may be taking over the helm at FCA

Last week a strong rumour surfaced that the Bank of England's Andy Haldane will become Martin Wheatley's replacement as CEO at the Financial Conduct Authority (FCA). Could this be true and would he be taking on a "mission impossible"?

The answer to the former is I really hope so and, like the A Team of the TV series, he and selected colleagues can surely prevail.

The prospect of Haldane stepping into the FCA's hot seat is hugely exciting. He is, arguably, the brightest star in the UK financial firmament. He totally gets the importance of equity investing and crowdfunding, as well as SMEs. On the other hand, the recidivists at the FCA don't understand the first, are terrified of the second and are not interested in the third. Haldane would not just be a breath of fresh air at North Colonnade, he would be a veritable tornado.

Obviously Haldane's speeches haven't had the attention that any pronouncements that Mark Carney or George Osborne are given, so it is well worth highlighting some of his thoughts here.

In a speech he made in April 2014 at the London Business School, Haldane drew attention to the fact that, thanks to the absurdity of accounting and regulatory requirements, UK institutional pension funds had cut equity holdings from 50 per cent in the late 1980s to under ten per cent today. The consequences for our economy are dire.

To quote Haldane: "The consequences of de-equitisation, for the financial system and the wider economy, may be just as dreadful as the word itself. Equity does a much better job than debt of sharing risk between borrowers and lenders as repayment terms adjust automatically with servicing capacity. Equity is also better able to support the financing of long-term investment projects because it is perpetual. So a world without equity is likely to be one with poorer risk-sharing and weaker long-term investment."

Of course every time bond (debt) yields go down the regulator demands that the pension fund manager buys yet more bonds to cover the further income shortfall. This is an absurdity that would sit very well at The Mad Hatter's Tea Party, but nowhere else. It is not beyond possibility that Haldane, once installed at the FCA, can break this spell once and for all.

But the good news doesn't stop there. In an interview with the Independent back in December 2012 Haldane made a series of incredibly enlightened statements on the future of SME funding. He started by observing: "The mono-banking culture that has existed since the 1990s is in retreat. We are now seeing a much more diverse eco-system springing up with new non-bank groups offering peer-to peer lending and crowd-funding, a more flexible way for companies to raise equity from angels."

He then went on to warm the cockles of my heart (and many others no doubt), but must have sent a shudder through the dinosaurs at the FCA, when he said: "I am congenitally pessimistic about most things in life, but on this I am really optimistic: it's a time of opportunity knocking for finance. Hopefully, the growth of peer-to-peer lenders, such as Zopa, Funding Circle and Thin Cats – and those involved in crowdfunding, such as Crowdcube – will help solve the problems we have in the UK with lending for SMEs."

But he didn't stop there. Just to make sure no one could be in any doubt about how he expected finance to change, he concluded: "These companies are tiny today but so was Google a decade-and-a-half ago. IT has changed every other industry such as film, music and even football clubs, so why not finance? With open access to borrower information – which is held centrally and virtually – there is no reason why end-savers and end-investors cannot connect directly."

I can only conclude that Haldane would change the culture and financial understanding immeasurably for the better. Such a transformation would work wonders for the growth of our economy. However, would he be allowed to? Would the entrenched recidivists in North Colonnade smother him? Well either a bit of luck has come along, or possibly the wily George Osborne has made that luck. It just so happens that three of the most senior FCA board members have reached the end of their tenure.

One of these is the very strange Mick McAteer, who I have on record as saying that he does not believe the typical consumer is very good at managing longevity of risk and that is why annuities are wonderful – oh dear! Another is Sir Brian Pomeroy, who has stoutly defended the FCA's foot dragging on releasing the report into the HBOS fiasco.

THE CITY GRUMP RIDES OUT

Headhunters have been appointed to find replacements. No doubt George Osborne will be consulted! Add in the judicious removal of one or two of the Executive (may I recommend Christopher Woolard), and Haldane's mission doesn't look so impossible

9 August 2016

FTSE 100 pay and the BHS pension fund deficit: Much less than six degrees of separation

In a report just out from the High Pay Unit it is noted that FTSE 100 CEOs enjoy average remuneration of £5.5m a year, which has increased by ten per cent in the last year. Let me explain the dismaying connection between this state of affairs and the, by now, infamous BHS pension fund deficit.

Back in September 2013 I highlighted the absurdly high levels of pay many senior executives were receiving and how this would lead to the cancer of socialism spreading once more. Sadly this is exactly what has happened. Jeremy Corbyn has taken over the Labour Party and our new prime minister has wasted no time in vowing a corporate crackdown on the privileged few. I suppose I should be pleased with the latter development but that would be to miss the root cause of what has happened and that is all to do with asset management and the structure of our pension funds.

The answer is to be found in the latest release from the Office for National Statistics: "Ownership of UK quotedshares". Go back to 1998 and you find our pension funds holding 22 per cent of their assets in UK quoted equities, whereas in 2014 this fell to a microscopic 3 per cent. The next largest professional fund manager category, insurance companies also held 22 per cent in 1998 and now have a paltry 6 per cent in our mainstream companies. There are a number of shockingly inevitable consequences of this but for the purpose of this article let's focus on two.

The first is that if your fund manager has an insignificant part of his assets tied up in our biggest companies he/she is not going to spend any time developing a constructive steward-like dialogue with FTSE 100 CEOs – and of course one of the consequences of such is that the boards of these companies can and do pay themselves egregious amounts of money. Some 54 per cent of shareholders are now from the "Rest of the World", as the ONS amusingly puts it, and a further 12 per cent are held by individuals; neither category are in a practical position to control excess.

The other inevitable consequence, which could be labelled the BHS effect, is highlighted in a brilliant article by Anthony Hilton in the Evening Standard. I can do no better than quote his succinct account of the disaster that has become our pension fund policy: "Until the 90s, the health of a pension fund was assessed by working out the value of the current and future income streams generated by the fund – basically the dividend flows – over the following 25 years. As long as this was more than what would have to be paid out, all was well. Then some bright spark of an accounting purist decided dividends were too volatile to be used as a long-term measure so the only income that could be assumed to be permanent was the 'risk-free' rate on government bonds or something similar.

"But doing the sums this way assumes pension funds earn much less money than is actually being earned. So it turns hitherto healthy funds into basket cases. And as each successive fall in interest rates pushes the risk-free rate even lower, things get worse.

"Then they hit on a cure that was worse than the disease – something called liability-driven investment. This means funds should give up trying to invest wisely for growth and focus instead on stopping things getting any worse. Funds can do this by buying bonds so as to hedge against future interest rate falls. This may convey the illusion of safety – but it is an illusion because liability-driven investment in the current climate is the most costly way imaginable to fund future retirement."

Last week the most dangerous man in Britain, Mark Carney, added to this financial fiasco by lowering interest rates, sending the BHS pension fund and all the other deficits spiralling upwards yet again.

Theresa May and Phillip Hammond have the tools to put an end to this shambles. Legislation should be passed to re-instate the equity dividend stream as being a core part of pension fund actuarial calculations. The common sense justification for this should be obvious. As the government relies on companies to grow its income so more wealth is distributed to finance public expenditure over the long term. Accordingly, income in the form of company dividends must also be recognised as a reliable contributor to pension funds over the long term.

As a result our quoted companies would return to mainstream pension fund asset allocation. Pension fund managers would have to re-engage with FTSE 100 boards as they always used to, and very soon absurd remuneration and unserviceable BHS-type deficits will be confined to the history books. Come on May and Hammond, you can do it. Be brave.

19 April 2017

Cheap labour is the curse of our times

One of the key tenets of the liberal establishment, and no doubt we shall be fed much more of this in the current election campaign, is cheap labour is essential for the smooth functioning of the UK and other advanced economies. They are oh so wrong.

My wife and I often visit friends in South Africa but each time we go we are more and more shocked by the graphic effects of an endless supply of extraordinarily cheap labour.

A straight forward example for you. We spent a few days in the very pleasant seaside resort of Wilderness on the beautiful Garden Route. There we were amazed to see some men digging out with shovels the foundations for a new apartment block. Not a JCB in sight. Why? Because the cost of a general labourer in sterling terms is just £2.50 a day.

Much of Africa continues under the slough of corruption and South Africa is seen as the honey pot. It naturally attracts enormous levels of unskilled immigrants in search of something better, thus continuously depressing wage rates. The result of all this is that the white Afrikaans, together with a smattering of fortunate indigenous blacks, have grown lazy and inefficient and why should they be otherwise, given they have an endless supply of cheap labour to do their every bidding?

An extreme example maybe but I suggest there are elements of South Africa's situation that have come to pass here in the UK. We can see this in agriculture and the hospitality industries where howls of anguish can be heard at the prospect of Brexit turning off the tap of cheap labour from Romania to Poland.

But should we listen? Step forward William Chip from the Center for Immigration Studies, Washington DC.

In a letter to the Financial Times he wrote: "In the 1997 report of the National Academy of Sciences to the US Commission on Immigration Reform (appointed by Democratic president Bill Clinton), the most exhaustive effort in American history (was made) to arrive at a fact-based, non-partisan foundation for immigration policy. A 2016 version of the report has been summarised in a 'User's Guide' by Harvard professor George Borjas, one of its contributors.

"According to the guide, current immigration flows are estimated to increase the income of native-born Americans by $50bn (about three-tenths of one per cent of total GDP). However, because historically high levels of immigration have lowered wages by five per cent, that £50bn net benefit is accompanied by an annual wealth transfer from employees to employers of $500bn, which helps explain the 'xenophobia' of president Donald Trump's working-class supporters. What employee would be comforted to learn his $500 pay cut made his boss $550 richer?"

So academic research suggests the benefits of cheap labour to most of us are a mirage. A persistent user of unskilled immigrants is the agricultural crop picking industry. It protests that it must have a steady supply of such or we won't get our strawberries but that line of reasoning can only breed inefficiency, low productivity and dulled entrepreneurialism. As night follows day, when that cheap labour is taken away, the more dynamic industry leaders will automate, productivity will shoot up and we will all wonder what the fuss was about.

Of course automation is not so easy to achieve in the hospitality industry but I suggest here things have become artificially cheap. A good example of this is a survey by Manchester University (reported in the Daily Telegraph) which has found we no longer think that going out to eat is anything special. Indeed the researchers found eating at a pub carvery or an Italian restaurant has come to be regarded as a cheaper and easier option to cooking at home.

Where does it say in Thomas Paine's seminal work, "The Rights of Man", that it is every Englishman's inalienable right to dine out every day of the week (I hesitate to say British as everything in Scotland is subsidised anyway, so may not apply up there)? If the end of cheap labour means that restaurant/pub prices have to increase so be it. The good will survive and we will value the experience.

Finally, we come full circle to the South African experience. Yesterday through the door popped a leaflet drawing my attention to a planning application from a nearby polytunnel operator to install 20 static mobile homes/caravans to house 80 pickers and security staff. South Africa is of course awash with shanty dwellings on the edge of towns servicing better off inhabitants therein. Is the same set up about to come here? Another reason to vote for Theresa May on June 8th.

15 March 2018

Rising interest rates finally explode the myth of your pension fund deficit

It's been a long time coming but finally reality is catching up with the "experts" who have been insisting that pension fund managers find the money to stuff their portfolios with more and more bonds to address so-called actuarial deficits.

It is a scandal perpetrated by the Pension Industry Regulator, egged on by pension fund consultants, the Bank of

England (BoE) and the FCA. Many heads should roll for the damage it has done to the British economy and our pockets. No doubt the financial establishment will close ranks but they are losing credibility in the eyes of anyone who cares to look.

I like to think it was Anthony Hilton, writing in the Evening Standard in 2016, that first drew attention to "Our mad approach to pension deficits". He put the madness succinctly and with lucidity: "We are talking about a misallocation of capital on a truly heroic scale, running to tens if not hundreds of billions of pounds – sums that pose a threat to the wider economy.

"The origin of the problem is that accountants and actuaries decided that, when making estimates about the future, any pension fund should only count what it could be absolutely sure of achieving. In the investment world, convention has it that only the totally secure return on government bonds can be considered as certain – though this is itself a heroic assumption in an age of sovereign defaults.

"The yield on bonds is therefore used to calculate how much the assets of pension funds will grow. This determines how big the asset pot needs to be today if it is to grow big enough to pay the pensions in years to come. If there are not enough assets in the pot today, that shortfall is the deficit figure. It follows from this that every time interest rates fall, the assets will grow at a slower rate. You need more of them now to avoid a shortfall in future. Each cut compounds the problem."

Hilton's conclusion was suitably unforgiving: "How in a sane world did we get here? It was said about one of the more intractable disputes of the 19th century that only three people understood the Schleswig-Holstein question – one was dead, one was mad and one had forgotten the answer.

"You might apply the same to pension fund valuation. Yet such is the power of inertia, so entrenched is the status quo that even sane people think that they have no choice but to follow the rules of a mad system. The actuaries and accountants who started all this have a lot to answer for. It is time for them to go back to the drawing board."

Unsurprisingly his article set off a storm of protest in the actuarial and regulatory world. The general tenet of their huffing and puffing was how can a mere journalist be expected to understand the calculations needed to quantify what these deficits are? The man is a charlatan and should be ignored. Indeed he has been as the pensions world has staggered under ever increasing deficit figures. I should say that Hilton is no charlatan and the last journalist you could describe as 'mere'.

But then something happened. Interest rates are going up! And what has that done to defined benefit pension deficits? In just one month they have halved. The Pension Protection Fund's 7800 Index reported that across Britain's almost 6,000 defined benefit funds the combined deficit in January fell from £104bn to £51bn. At a stroke of a pen the pensions bogey is disappearing.

This mickey mouse accounting would be funny if it wasn't so serious. Earlier this month the BoE admitted, in a report it commissioned, that its QE induced driving down of interest rates had a knock-on effect on defined benefit pension fund schemes where liabilities rise when interest rates fall, thus increasing costs for employers backing the schemes. The BoE said that at one point the combined deficit reached 15 per cent of GDP.

It found that companies with large deficits paid lower dividends and companies required by the regulator to make deficit recovery contributions spent less on dividends and investment than other businesses.

Indeed the latest example of this induced strife is the lengthening strike by university lecturers over their pension scheme's deficit, which resulted in a letter published in the

FT from the former chief accountant of the mighty Railways Pension fund (RPMI Railpen), Dr Tim Wilkinson, and the immediate past president of the Institute of Chartered Secretaries and Administrators, Frank Curtiss.

To quote from their letter: "We think insufficient attention is being directed towards the regulatory framework. Actuarial and accounting standards, bolstered by several Pensions Acts, have become divorced from the economic reality of running a defined benefit scheme. The calculation of liabilities using bond rates exogenous to the pensions ecosystem, coupled with the statutory requirement to eliminate deficits quickly, can make schemes appear unaffordable when, even on prudent assumptions, they have healthy cash flows in perpetuity.

"The resulting deficits and costs are little more than accounting and actuarial illusions, but are made real by regulations. Employers balk at the expense, with the result that schemes are indirectly forced to close by the very regulations that are designed to protect them."

The absurdity of how our pension schemes are valued and the damage that has been done has been going on far too long. The myopia of those in charge of this vital industry is a scandal so heads should roll as reality dawns. Meanwhile the next time you are told you have a pension deficit that needs addressing ignore the false prophet.

CHAPTER 4

THE POWERS THAT BE

"The most dangerous man to any government is the man who is able to think things out for himself, without regard to the prevailing superstitions and taboos. Almost inevitably he comes to the conclusion that the government he lives under is dishonest, insane, and intolerable..."

H.L. Mencken

"Dear Government... I'm going to have a serious talk with you if I ever find anyone to talk to."

Stieg Larsson

For those of us who have had the privilege of wandering around the corridors of power from time to time it surely remains a mystery how anything gets done at all? Earnest looking civil servants appear in your meeting with some or other Minister. They dutifully scribble away taking notes. After an hour of this and a nice cup of tea everybody smiles and departs, having achieved precisely nothing. No wonder successful businessmen, attracted like moths to the light of vanity, find the apparatus of government a deathly experience.

In truth I suspect something only happens when the political imperative becomes so demanding that "action this day" crystallises. Witness the tortuous Brexit debate.

Being a political reporter must be one of the cushiest jobs in the world. There is just always so much material to work with. Here the City Grump joins in, constructively I trust.

20 December, 2010

The way out of a recession is to save, not spend

'The Consumer Failed to Deliver Last Year' is a digestible reprint of a book by Terry Arthur. It (unfashionably) argues that the way out of recession is to save, not spend.

On Googling "Terry Arthur", I instantly warmed to him when I discovered that he has written another book titled 'Crap: A Guide to Politics'. Definitely my kinda guy!

Mr Arthur's book starts with the tale of two workmen digging out a quarry with a gigantic excavator. One said to the other: "It's a crying shame. This quarry would provide work for a thousand men with shovels". The other replied: "Or a million men with teaspoons." The excavator has enabled 1,000 men to work with greater productivity (and thus greater rewards); two of them in a quarry and the rest elsewhere. How did the excavator get there? As Mr Arthur points out, it was built by abstinence. Someone, somewhere, decided to abstain from consumption to build it or have it built. Had this not occurred, shovels at best and bare hands at worst would have been the order of the day

The lesson is that savings, not consumption, bring riches. To quote from the book: "For an individual, this is not controversial. Nor is it for a household. But Margaret Thatcher was accused of being dangerously simplistic for extending the argument to a whole nation and exhorting it to practise good housekeeping." In Germany, Angela Merkel has taken up the same theme much to the disgust of Keynesian groupies worldwide.

Across the pond, clearly Mr Bernanke – aided and abetted by Washington – takes the diametrically opposite view. There they are doing everything they can (QE, continuing tax handouts for the rich and new spending programmes) to get the consumer to spend, spend, spend.

Most economists would have you believe that such government pump priming eventually lifted the US out of the depression in the thirties, whereas actually what came to their rescue was WWII. The massive demands of war meant that Americans were forced to save and, at the same time, build better, more productive capital equipment. One-nil to Mr Arthur, methinks. Let's hope it doesn't take a war to bring profligate Western governments to their senses this time around.

3 March, 2011

Why a big bank split-up makes sense

Two newspapers recently ran very different but intriguing articles on splitting up the banks. Here's my take.

The first comes from London's Evening Standard and confirms my worst fears about the spineless expediency of our Chancellor. The paper reports on the events leading up to the deal (ironically known as Merlin, who was always a dab hand with the smoke and mirrors) between the government and the bankers that emerged last month.

Their sources suggest that Osborne offered to rein in the Vickers Commission on banking in return for striking a better deal on bonuses. The major banks are scared stiff that Vickers will recommend their high-street banking activities be separated from their highly lucrative investment banking activities, thus preventing the one fuelling the other.

According to the Evening Standard, when Vickers heard about Osborne's manoeuvring, the entire committee threatened to resign thus forcing him to back off. So, for the sake of grabbing a few headlines on bonuses, our doughty Chancellor appears to have been happy to sacrifice the possibility of preventing the banks from running off with our money in future. Sad and pathetic.

The other article was an interview in the Daily Telegraph with Anders Bouvin (the UK chief executive of the Swedish bank Svenske Handelsbanken) who draws attention to the fact they make lending commitments in the deeply unfashionable way of letting their branch managers take the decisions. Head office confines itself to being the support centre. To quote: "we are different, even in Sweden. This boils down to a fundamental humanist view. We believe that if you put trust in people, people will respond in a positive way and take responsibility and deliver results that they would not have achieved in a command and control environment." Bouvin admits it sounds "corny" but it's not just flaky ideology: "96 per cent of all credit transactions are taken by the branch managers. Handelsbanken couldn't be more different to a UK high-street bank. When do you meet a decision maker at a high-street branch?"

So I suggest that if you yearn for the days when your bank had an understanding of your business and you were able to talk to someone sensible at a local level about such, get down to one of Mr Bouvin's 97 UK branches. As the paper observes, Handelsbanken has delivered better than average returns for the 39 years since this policy was implemented and has emerged from the two crises, in 1992 and 2008, unscathed.

Keep your fingers crossed that Vickers doesn't lose his nerve. Getting our banks to run their high-street banking entirely separately from volatile investment banking could be the first step towards regaining a safer, sensible, Handelsbanken way of doing business.

16 December, 2011

2011: the year of smoke and mirrors

Let's look back at 2011, a year when those in power sought to use as much smoke and mirrors as possible to keep the truth from their citizens.

The longest running smoke screen is, of course, Quantitative Easing. A particular favourite as it keeps interest rates artificially low by creating a bull market in UK government debt. This is, of course, all too good to be true. As the Telegraph points out: "By switching on the printing presses, the Bank of England, which is 100% owned by Her Majesty's Government, is buying up a third of the debt owed by Her Majesty's government. The Treasury is becoming ever more in debt to itself. It's as strange as that.

Luckily for Mervyn and Dave, the situation has become so bad in the Eurozone that the bond vigilantes continue to regard this fiction as the lesser of two evils when confronted with the prospect of the wholesale collapse of the Club Med countries. Not surprising, then, that the beleaguered boss of the Bank of France has just cried out in frustration at the apparently stronger credit rating of perfidious Albion. Don't worry Monsieur Noyer, we're unlikely to be able to keep the QE fiction going for much longer.

Back in July, I had the temerity to suggest that bank, airline and textile stocks should never feature on investors' buy lists. Not even I realised just what a terrible mess the banks would be in as they go into 2012.

The simple fact of the matter is most Euroland banks are bust – and ours would go down with them if it wasn't for two other giant smoke and mirror jobs that have been put up in the past month by the central banks. Namely, unlimited lending of dollars by the big three; and the ECB offering three year loans at one per cent to the region's banks.

These desperate actions perfectly demonstrate how bad things are. Markets are currently breathing a sigh of relief that the central bankers have responded to the cry of "do something, anything" but the illusion of activity won't last.

Back on the home front, the FSA has been belching clouds of smoke with its recently published 420-page report into the circumstances behind the demise of RBS. The appointment of an insider, in the shape of the ex-banker and regulator Sir David Walker, to stop the FSA hiding embarrassing facts was not encouraging. Unsurprisingly the FSA plumped for the old PR trick of a "Snow White job", deflecting criticism by apologising for being asleep at the wheel. This seems to have satisfied most commentators but gloriously misses the point, which is that first and foremost the FSA is a political body not an independent regulator.

It implemented the disastrous "light touch" banking

regulation because the government told it to. So long as it goes on wanting to keep politicians happy, it will be as much use as the proverbial chocolate teapot.

Lighter smokescreen and mirror moments were provided by News International and the Royal Wedding. It was most entertaining to watch the Murdoch clan trying to defend the indefensible, ranging from the physical acrobatics of Rupert's wife at the Select Committee hearing, to the mental ones of James as he continues to deny all knowledge of mass phone hackings.

The Royal Wedding reminded us all how good "The Firm" is at conjuring up fairytale princesses to take the nation's mind off the grizzly business of everyday living. Long may that continue.

There are, though, two little rays of light that can be spied through the smoke. Firstly Osborne & Co do seem to be exhibiting some understanding of the need to encourage equity investment into small companies with their widening of EIS and VCT criteria (NB: subject to Brussels approval!). Would it be too much to hope, though, that in 2012 CGT is abolished on trading in small cap stocks, thus instantly making a huge difference to liquidity and hence capital formation in this vital area of economic growth? The second ray of light is, of course, Dave plucking up courage to say no to Merkozy. This rickety cart drawn by the Merkozy pantomime horse threatens to run away with our interests and we are quite right to distance ourselves from it.

Well done, Dave. Just don't lose your bottle in 2012!

2012: A year of sporting heroes and establishment zeros

In a year when most of us lost any faith we might have had in the Establishment doing or getting anything right, wasn't it a real tonic to see those old fashioned values of hard work and dedication win through on the sporting scene? Thank you to our Olympians and other sporting teams for giving us some much needed good news.

Of course there was one key figure among "the powers that be" who put in her customary level of hard work and dedication thus standing, as usual, head and shoulders above the rest. The Queen, as head of The Firm, put in a peerless performance in her Diamond Jubilee year. Thank you, Ma'am.

Sadly, the rest of them should be sent to Room 101. The banks yet again plumbed the depths with routines that make Al Capone look a saint. Gigantic financial manipulation, money laundering, and mis-selling on a massive scale can only mean that we will have no respect for them for a very long time to come – and yet, they still don't get it.

Barclays elects an old City bigwig as chairman who immediately turns round and appoints the chief executive of the FSA – one Hector Sants, who was on the Regulatory bridge as all these appalling things were going on – as Head of Compliance. They decide to give a package of a mere £3m to boot.

But that's not all. In the New Year's Honours List they awarded him a Knighthood! Even that natural supporter of the Establishment, the Financial Times spluttered, "four years trying to right the wrongs of a previous decade should not earn entry to Buckingham Palace." Lord Oakeshott put it rather more venomously: "He was a very solid food manufacturing analyst at [stockbrokers] Phillips & Drew, but does he really need a knighthood now on top of his £3m package at the Barclays?"

Sorry Ma'am, clearly your ministers and advisors have learnt nothing.

Hardly surprising then that a sigh of relief went up from every quarter as an outsider was appointed the next Governor of the Bank of England. Sadly not that outside, of course, since he did do time with Goldman Sachs. Nevertheless, there are signs he may pursue a refreshingly forthright approach.

For example, he looks keen to abandon the fiction that the BoE is targeting an inflation rate of two per cent. With interest rates at near zero and inflation averaging north of three per cent for years now, he looks, instead, set to acknowledge that full scale financial repression is the name of the game.

Elsewhere, the BBC has managed to blow a hole in its image as the nation's ultimate bastion of respectability. Who would have thought a disc jockey could cause such chaos? Luckily for them the Leveson-exposed antics of News Corporation have prevented their main competitor from taking much advantage of Auntie's pain. Talking of Leveson, it is disturbing to watch the attempt of the legal establishment to seize the initiative in determining what our press can and can't do... which brings us to our prime minister.

Good to see Cameron has some courage when it comes to questioning Leveson. As Private Eye put it, we apologise if we may have given the impression that the prime minister was, "in some way a gutless coward who had failed to confront any serious issue with any degree of conviction and without recourse to a series of U-turns, indecision and shilly-shallying."

Could 2013 be the year when Dave finally asks us if we want to leave that ultimate example of a corrupt, self-serving, profligate, ineffectual, time-wasting establishment known as the EU?

You can tell that, despite everything, I remain a hopeless optimist…

9 May, 2013

Have you satisfied the State today?

It's been a while since I've come across the State at the sharp end but my experiences so far over helping crowdfunding come of age make me want to urge on the Nigel Farages and Beppe Grillos of our world.

The fledgling crowdfunding industry is feeling its way forward in how to satisfy the State. Should it fall into the arms of our labyrinthine regulator, or should it follow the instinct of those that say the crowd is perfectly capable of self-policing common sense ethical standards? Luckily we have identified a very astute member of parliament who is keen to help us climb the North Face. Said MP is in his eighth decade so he is not exactly short of experience.

An inner sanctum of the State is Portcullis House, opposite the Houses of Parliament. From the outside it looks like something out of Gotham City. From the inside you feel as if you've entered a bubble that knows, but is happy to be separate, from the world at large. It is, of course, where most MPs have their offices but it feels to me more like George Orwell's 1984 "Ministry of Thought".

One 21 year-old-student, Hannah Riley who visited it recently, described it thus, "it seemed to me Portcullis House is far from a microcosm of society and is instead politics' answer to the Stepford Wives" Spot on, Hannah.

Anyway, once past the very tight security –jackets off (though not yet shoes), everything scanned, a multiplicity of police with guns – we make it to a meeting room. There our trusty MP is waiting to assist. We have had several hours of meetings now and just about all that time has been taken up with debating just how are we going to satisfy the State?

Did Gottlieb Daimler on inventing the motor car, or Watson and Crick with DNA, or Tim Berners-Lee with the World Wide Web, think to themselves, "well, we'd better check with the authorities first before going ahead"? Nowadays it seems that our first reaction when bringing something new to people's lives is to work out how to prevent it being strangled by the many arms of the State. This is sickening.

Farage and Grillo have, of course, identified that our 21st century lives are being steered by an ever more expansive political elite safe in their bubbles at Portcullis House in London and the Berlaymont in Brussels. They are saying, why should we continue to put up with these cosseted elites telling us how to live our lives? In the words of Mrs Thatcher, it is time to say "no, no, no".

This is very scary for the establishment at large. Janan Garnesh, the Financial Times political columnist remarked with disdain "the personal appeal of Mr Farage, Kent's answer to Pierre Poujade, the mid-20th century French populist, has the knack of radiating clubbable good cheer while cursing almost everything about modern life". If this is the best the critics can come up with then Farage will certainly be no mirage in the next General Election.

In many ways, crowdfunding provides the perfect test as to whether a very modern phenomenon, being the internet-based mass funding of companies, can avoid the long arm of State interference. So far, some of the crowdfunding platforms have already surrendered to the embrace of the Financial

Conduct Authority. Others are hoping they can find sufficient sympathisers on the inside of our dystopian system to ensure common sense democratic self- regulation wins through. We shall know who has prevailed by the end of this year.

18 June, 2013

Is Cameron spending our money well?

Our prime minister has been doing his top table bit at this week's G8 and a speech on the EU a few days ago, but is this a productive use of our money and his time?

In a speech given in deepest Essex, David Cameron announced that a key part of his international ambitions for the UK "is our place at the top table. At the UN. The Commonwealth. NATO. The G8. The G20 and, yes – the EU." This inspired a wonderful cartoon by Christian Adams in the Telegraph depicting Cameron as the Sunday joint waiting to be carved up by Merkel, Hollande and Barroso, accompanied by the headline: "We have to be at the Top Table".

Quite apart from rushing out to buy the original cartoon from Adams, it got me thinking about the costs and benefits of Cameron's expansiveness.

The benefits are always, obviously, stated as Britain gains from being up there with the world's biggest political beasts as it means we can influence events to our economic advantage. Anything else? No, this rather airy fairy argument is about it.

Some of the costs are, sadly, on display as we play host to the current G8 summit. It is taking place in a hotel that no one wants to buy from the receiver, next to a town whose closed high street businesses have been repainted with fake shopfronts, and the agenda primarily consists of whether our little island gets involved in stepping up the bloody and vile shooting match in Syria, Lebanon, et al. Has all the ingredients of a classic Shakespearean tragedy, doesn't it?

Too often being at the top table seems to require us to supply an endless stream of expensive manpower and weaponry to any and every civil war hotspot. We are propelled into this position because history suggests that our economic superiors in the form of Germany, Japan and China cannot be trusted to do the right thing. So you and I are expected to carry on paying out huge sums of money to have our children shot at wherever it pleases the top table to send them. Do you get the feeling that Obama and Putin are laughing at the financial and human bind we are in? I do.

What about our financial pulling power? Our politicians continue to convince themselves we have the economic clout to get GB taken seriously at the top table. The facts are not with Cameron and Co. Our GDP per capita puts us at number eight in the world and even that is misleading as, although China and Russia are lower down the rankings, no one would suggest that the countries of the world are going to listen to us ahead of them.

At least with our situation in Europe there is a growing understanding amongst Britons that the cost of being at that particular top table is, as the Adam's cartoon so perfectly puts it, humiliatingly high. If we can get Downing Street and Westminster to understand that then our dosh may soon no longer be wasted on the top tables' tosh.

30 August, 2013

The poodle finds its voice

The Prime Minister lost the debate over whether to join in the "punishment" of Assad last night but actually something far more important for our nation will ensue.

Isn't it interesting that all the reported speeches concentrated on 'do we have enough evidence to ensure that the WMD mistakes of Iraq are not repeated?' The conscious mood was that we must have nigh on 100 per cent certainty before we join in hurling our (limited) stock of cruise missiles at chemical weapons plants.

Subconsciously though, the "no" vote represented something far, far, more important. It reflected that the majority of British citizens at long last understand we are a smallish trading nation off the north coast of Europe and, as such, we should stop pretending otherwise. For years we have been in a humiliating transitory phase between a great superpower and becoming another trading entity. The manifestation of this changing status is because our political and military establishment has chosen, for most of my 60 years on this planet, to act as the world leader's poodle, which comes running whenever the White House says so.

Many MPs may not fully realise it yet but what they did last night in Westminster was to say our poodle days are drawing to a close. It took the absurdity of the Syrian situation to do so. Prime Minister David Cameron recalls Parliament to discuss how we can ensure that the Assad regime kills people nicely. Short of paying to send all its insurgents to the Dignitas clinic in Switzerland there is no known way of killing your population nicely. The BBC, in another attempt to stir up hypocritical outrage, ran a piece during the vote on how a Syrian school was napalmed recently while conveniently forgetting to mention that the White House napalmed away in Vietnam whenever it suited them to do so.

The front page of today's Telegraph gives a perfect display of the passing of old Britain. The headline is "No to war, blow to Cameron" and is accompanied by an enormous picture of an RAF Typhoon, an aircraft that was eventually delivered hopelessly over budget and at vast expense to the electorate.

Perhaps now the Britain we hand onto our children's generation will be one that spends more time and money on building a fruitful economic base for its occupants than one that squanders political and financial capital in trying to keep up with the world's de facto superpower. I think Westminster is beginning to get our message.

5 January 2017

Will 2017 be the year our country awakes from a quarter century of slumber?

It all started 27 years ago when the incoming prime minister, John Major, said he was aiming for "a nation at ease with itself". After the revolutionary shocks of Thatcherism he rightly perceived the nation wanted to draw the proverbial duvet over its head and comfort itself with "warm beer and cricket". The scene was set for the rise of mediocrity – and we hope things change for 2017.

After Major came the oleaginous Tony Blair who managed to whisper sweet nothings into the nation's ear for a whole decade

– he said, "I'm a pretty straight sort of guy" in an interview in 2007.

A man whose judgement of international players was so bad he remained in awe of George Bush, became a godfather to one of Rupert Murdoch's infants in a white robed ceremony on the banks of the River Jordan, and in his retirement years aligned himself with colourful characters from former communist countries.

Then, finally, we were given David Cameron, almost a professional slumberer in his own right. He was the apotheosis of that Etonian desire to make governing look languidly effortless. The trouble was that he believed his own publicity and made little effort on anything, The EU being a prime example.

Former prime minister Harold Macmillan, in a sentence criticised for its Jew-consciousness, remarked of Margret Thatcher's cabinet that it "had more old Estonians than old Etonians". My, how the wheel came full circle, with no less than 12 members of that famous school in Cameron's line-up. And thanks, in considerable part, to these three men and their acolytes, for more than a quarter of a century now we have become, what is known in financial circles as "risk–off". We have become obsessed with measuring/testing everything in an effort to mitigate risk.

The result is that our NHS is swarming with managers measuring away and contributing nothing of worth to the nation's health, our education system is staffed up to produce test data geared only to preparedness for the next OFSTED inspection, and the growth industry that has left all others for dead is compliance.

In our risk-off country mediocrity has paid very well indeed for those at the top. A study published by Lancaster University Management School just before January 2017 found that in the 11 years to 2014 the median pay package of FTSE 350 directors had increased by 82 per cent to £1.5m whereas the return on invested capital (net of the cost of capital) had been just 8.5 per cent.

This risk-off culture of mediocrity as John Hegarty, creative founder of the famous Bartle Bogle Hegarty agency, points out has spread to that most dynamic of industries, advertising. In an article for the FT published two days into 2017 and under the heading "Daring rather than data will save advertising," he said: "It would be wonderful if we could simply feed a number of assumptions into a databank and wait for the suggested actions. Indeed, many marketing professionals believe that is the future-predictable, assured and safe. But life is not like that and neither is marketing.

"Steve Jobs or James Dyson did not build brilliant companies by waiting for a set of algorithms to tell them what to do. They built those companies by backing their own beliefs, innovating with technology that changed the way we think and behave, and then communicating those beliefs through the use of broadcast and other media. Persuasion and promotion."

Indeed a quarter of a century of slumbering governments lumbering us with a plethora of over endowed entities of indifferent ability was perfectly rounded off with David Cameron's resignation honours list. In among 46 gongs handed out were peerages for 13 of his advisors, some of whom are barely in long trousers and all of whom are failures by dint of his resignation. Not forgetting the OBE for Samantha Cameron's stylist who I suppose did at least have the quality of keeping her looking pretty to the end.

But hark! 2017 dawns with the country waking up to the invigorating task of shaking off the largest stupefying presence of them all, the EU. Is Theresa May up to pulling the sword from the stone? There are some encouraging signs. Some of the old school are now leaving. At the time of writing our EU ambassador, Ivan Rogers, has resigned whilst penning a note to his staff urging them to carry on his fight, so no professionalism there then but it is what we have come to expect from such people.

The real test though is about to come. By now it must be clear on either side of the Brexit debate that it will be a complete waste of time attempting to hammer out some kind of deal with Brussels et al. Just like our leaders of the last 27 years they are masters of the art of can kicking and obfuscation. Come March when May exercises Article 50 we must say to the 27 remaining countries: "We are leaving with no pre-conditions. If in the next two years you wish to negotiate on certain elements of interest to you our door is, of course, open."

Will May have the courage to wake us from our slumber? I hope so. It is time to move from risk off to risk-on.

10 March 2017

Would the Treasury be more at home with Jeremy Corbyn?

Judging by this week's omnishambles Budget, the Treasury would indeed be more at home with Jeremy Corbyn.

It is as if the Treasury has forgotten everything those strong Tory chancellors, Nigel Lawson and Ken Clarke, drummed into them. The State is not there to take an ever increasing slice of its citizens' income.

Sadly chancellor Philip Hammond is not in the same league as Messrs Lawson and Clarke. He lacks their imagination and common sense. He is no better and no worse than some middle ranking director in a FTSE 350 company.

He is most certainly not equipped to deal with a Treasury that has slipped back into the bad old ways of Michael Foot and the Corbynistas whose La La Land existence consists of a state that always knows best and therefore has a divine right to extract ever more taxpayer money to satisfy its omnificence. Hardly surprising as the current generation of Treasury officials have been brought up at the knee of Brussels, which is, of course, the supreme example of the "we know what's good for you" sausage machine.

Understandably and rightly so the mainstream media has latched on to the contradiction of a Tory government that is never slow to extol the virtues of self- made resilience, which then turns round and delivers, as the Budget centrepiece mark you, a cut to the earning ability of its natural supporters. This state of affairs is about as badly thought out as it is possible to be and can be laid squarely at the door of a second rate chancellor advised by a semi-Red Treasury.

But it gets worse. Much worse. For a while it looked as if those in La La Land were beginning to grasp that as a populace we cannot go on racking up more debt, nationally and personally, and the time had come to understand the virtues of equity capital. A whole host of influential commentators and financiers have been pointing this out for a year or more now. Indeed even the Treasury is talking about the need for "patient capital" and over in the US they are beginning to seriously address the damaging tax advantages given to debt over equity. So what does "Spreadsheet Phil" and his advisors do? They administer a cut to tax-free dividend income. For my money it is not so much the cost to people's pockets of this action, it is the sheer lack of joined up thinking and undoubtedly proves that neither the Treasury nor this government has any interest at all in encouraging long term equity capital formation. In other words they are anti-capitalist. Corbyn and Co must be delighted.

What to do? Firstly Hammond must be sacked forthwith. We cannot have a laughing stock of a chancellor when it comes to squaring up to Article 50. To use language the Treasury would clearly understand, a swathe of officials should be purged and replaced by civil servants from the Department for Business, Energy and Industrial Strategy who at least stand a chance of having some empathy with those who are trying to move this country away from a state presence that only knows how to say "feed me".

21 June 2017

Britain today: Political pygmies versus Marxist malcontents

The eye-popping outturn of the general election combined with subsequent events I am sure makes most of us despair of our political classes. What is going on in Britain today and what can be done?

There are many views on what went wrong for the Conservatives – and Britain today – on 8 June. Mine is that Jeremy Corbyn and Co brilliantly managed to galvanise 18-24 year olds into the polling booths with the promise to axe much hated (rightly in my view) student fees/loans.

You only have to look at the results in university areas such as Canterbury (held by the Tories for 100 years), Sheffield Hallam (bye, bye, students' favourite target, Nick Clegg) and Southampton to see this at work.

Add in prime minister Theresa May's refusal to allow her MPs to campaign nationally and hey presto a horrifying collection of Trotskyists and other Marxists come within a hair's breadth of seizing the levers of power.

Indeed the actions of and pronouncements from the Labour leadership in Britain today conjures up a vision of current Venezuela, interspersed with scenes from Dr Zhivago. How can 40 per cent of our voting citizenry fall for the Hugo Chavez/Nicolás Maduro doctrine that we can spend our way to happiness by taxing the "wealthy"? Very easily, because our education system has never, ever, regarded it of any importance to produce financially literate pupils.

The result is that we send our children out into the world with no idea how to manage their own income let alone with any knowledge of wider financial issues. Easy meat for Corbyn's Marxist malcontents to prey on as the Conservatives are now finding out. Accordingly it is imperative that from now on, at GCSE stage, the young must be taught/ introduced to the world of finance.

They must learn money trees can only be planted in unforgiving soil and wither quickly. They must be taught how wealth is generated. They must learn the advantages of equity finance compared with debt. They must learn what part the State can play without permanently damaging its citizens.

Meantime up comes a chilling scene straight from Dr Zhivago. Last week's devastating fire in a North Kensington high rise turned out, among other things, to produce a vile reaction from Corbyn who, when discussing the re-housing of those from Grenfell Tower, went into full Marxist "property is theft" speak, when asked by ITV interviewer Robert Peston if he would "seize it forever, or just take it for as long as it's needed".

He replied: "Occupy, compulsory purchase it, requisition it, there's a lot of things you can do."

And what are our political pygmies, formerly known as the Conservative Party, doing to counter all of this? They are spending their time obsessing about how long should they give May as prime minister? The arch player of this sad little game in Britain today is of course the newly enthroned editor of the London Evening Standard, the no longer Right Honourable George Osborne.

This man who has little to crow about in his time in Downing Street (indeed we are all still suffering from his appointment of our unimpressive BoE governor, Mark Carney) now spends his time using the organ he has been given to pour a continuous stream of bile onto May. A more irresponsible strategy is hard to imagine at this time.

Any Conservative who wants to become leader of the party and government must first win his/her spurs by getting in front of the nation and successfully demolishing the Marxist confidence tricksters that have now become Her Majesty's official opposition.

Until the people of the UK can see this happening there will be no confidence in a replacement for our current prime minister. It is no use the likes of Boris Johnson just calling Corbyn "a mutton-headed mugwump". The nation demands much more than name calling. It demands education.

20 December 2017

2017: The year of economic naivety

The bibliophile and author, Anatole France, once said: "It is well for the heart to be naïve and the mind not to be." Britain in 2017 has seen far too many examples of economic naivety – the heart ruling the head.

The grandmammy of all economic naivety examples from 2017 has to be Theresa May's snap election campaign back in early summer. Her naivety was her belief that she alone was the key to trouncing the Corbynistas. Her experienced cabinet colleagues and many other Conservatives would be barely seen or heard, merely confined to tramping round their constituency doorsteps. The result was political carnage and she and us are condemned to keep living with the consequences.

That general election did throw up another highly significant example of naivety and cunning. I mean of course Jeremy Corbyn assuring student voters that his party would do away with their having to find the money for university education. Sadly most students are financially illiterate and protestations by Amber Rudd that there is " no magic money tree" (a subject she probably knows something about, having had a father who was struck off as a company director) fell on deaf ears, with the result that many key constituencies in England swung to Labour. It is amusing to note that in Scotland, where university education is free, the Tories did very well indeed.

Amazingly the economic naivety over student fees and the ensuing debt rolls on and on. The most stunning example of this occurred last month when David "two-brains" Willetts, the former universities minister who orchestrated raising tuition fees to £9,000 a year, said that he never envisaged inflation would hit three per cent when devising the mechanism (RPI plus three per cent) used to calculate the interest rate applied to student debt, now running at 6.1 per cent. Perhaps he really does come from another planet because if he was from this one he would know that average inflation in the UK for the last 100 years has been running at....three per cent!

As an aside here, it is good to see that at long last, even though it is too late for Willetts, a real effort is being made to educate our financially naive children. Last month, the Open University, with funding partly from the Chartered Accountants Livery Company and its dynamic master, Clive Parritt, launched a major initiative to teach 16-18 year-olds in schools about personal financial management.

I suppose, naturally, the ongoing saga about our relationship with the EU post-Brexit, whenever that might happen, is pregnant with naivety. There are two strands at work here. One is that ardent "remainers" cling to the belief that the EU is worth fighting for when in reality it remains in a complete pickle of an unsustainable structure. As Wolfgang Munchau wrote on 18 December, in the fanatically pro-remain Financial Times, in his article "Recovery cannot hide the holes in the Eurozone": "We end the year in perfect gridlock. The proposal of the German finance ministry is unacceptable to the French and the Italians. The French proposal is unacceptable to the European Commission. The Commission's proposal is unacceptable to everybody. As is [Martin] Schulz's idea of a United States of Europe.

"Will Eurozone reform happen eventually? If it does, then it will not be through an ordinary political process but another crisis, one that threatens the wealth of northern creditor nations. This is the real cliff edge Europe faces. Not Brexit."

The other main strand of naivety is that Brexiteers, much of the media, and presumably much of the electorate, seem to think that May's recent 4am dash to Brussels, Neville Chamberlain style, has achieved rather more than Chamberlain did with Hitler back in 1938. The fact is in both cases the key players have yet again signed up to the European tradition of kicking the can down the road.

"Nothing is agreed until everything is agreed," maybe a neat phrase but the subtext is obviously that nothing has been agreed by anyone about anything. When the great British public wake up to this, there are going to be fireworks.

Into this unappetising scene lumbers, stage right, the previously sacked attorney general, one Dominic Grieve, who decided that the time had come to give his fine legal training an airing by putting down a successful parliamentary motion rebelling against his party's Brexit process. In his show of legal conviction it clearly has not occurred to him that he has run straight into the welcoming arms of Corbyn's stormtroopers at Momentum who care not one fig for the niceties of parliamentary democracy, but do know how to go about constructing a Marxist state. His political naivety is breathtaking.

And, finally, what of my own naivety I hear you say? Well, the latest example is I have just shelled out £610 for my annual subscription to the Financial Times in the belief that our only national financial newspaper has an interest in covering news and developments in British Companies. Considering back in 2012 I wrote a City Grump entitled "Has the FT given up on British businesses?" this is stunningly naive. Indeed, just how so was rubbed into me this morning as the Lex column, that hallowed home of former distinguished alumni such as Nigel Lawson, Richard Lambert, Martin Taylor and David Freud, today chose not to cover one single UK item. Oh dear.

I wish you a Happy Christmas and a New Year ruled more by the mind.

July 31 2018

The great university swindle: A Westminster/ Whitehall production

The much trumpeted university student fees and loans concoction is bringing on a scandal of biblical proportions. It embraces fraudulent government accounting, a debased admissions system and an army of disillusioned and over indebted graduates. I have a modest proposal.

What the government in the form of the usual ne'er-do

well, the Treasury, is up to beggars belief. I am indebted (sic) to Neil Collins who wrote a succinct analysis of, as he puts it, 'an accounting sleight of hand no fraudster can match,' in the Financial Times recently.

The House of Lords Economic Affairs Committee in June described the student loans system as 'the pyramid of fiscal illusions in the treatment of student finance.'

Collins explains how it works: 'The loan accrues interest (at RPI plus 3 per cent) which the government counts as income, even though none is received. The inevitable loss of capital (and accrued income) is not accounted for until the loan is written off decades hence.'

'The 2017/18 cohort, for example, produces an 'income' of roughly £1 billion a year until 2050. When the remaining loans are written off there's a whacking £25 billion charge over the following three years. This is just for one year's loans.'

That leaves a problem when the debt can rolling down the road eventually comes to rest in 2050, but the tricksters at the Treasury have thought of that as they have started selling off the loan book at less than 50 per cent of face value. This is deemed to be a 'holding loss,' which surprise, surprise does not affect the government deficit.

This is fraud on a grand scale. Currently student loans are £100 billon or just under 5 per cent of GDP. Yet another reason then for the voting public, when they find out about such a thing, to regard our political and financial elite with contempt.

So what's happening at the entry level to this infernal machine? Universities, aware that they are too many in number, are now handing out a massive 67,915 unconditional offers to students as compared to just 2,985 in 2013.

Sam Gyimah, the Universities Minister, has accordingly accused universities of acting in a 'completely irresponsible' manner, urging them to cut down on this shameful practice.

'Places at universities should only be offered to those who will benefit from them, and giving out unconditional offers just to put bums on seats undermines the credibility of the university system,' he said.

Go to the top of the class Mr Gyimah.

Now the 'in demand' school kid has arrived at the university of choice, what does he/she make of it? Well in the three years of attending these so-called seats of learning the student might notice the university vice chancellor is doing very nicely, thank you, on £400k plus a year and that a massive 33% of his fellow 18-year-olds are also studying for something or other .

Does the by now highly indebted student grow into a happy graduate? Absolutely not. In a survey this month of London graduates by Barclays Bank it found that nearly half of those graduates see their student years as a bad investment.

As the Telegraph reported: 'The regretful ex-students were dismayed to find that,contrary to widespread lore, they were not actually any more employable with degree in hand, and to add insult to injury, they were left with average debts of £50,000."

What an unholy mess. Fraudulent loan accounting, farcical admission procedures and disillusioned graduates. It is now an inescapable fact that there are far too many university places sucking up far too much cash leading to sharp practice and ill equipped, financially handicapped generations of young people.

What can be done? The answer to that question is obvious. Shut half these 'educational' establishments, refurbish the vast number of student accommodation blocks that have sprung up all over our cities into much needed affordable housing, thereby making huge inroads into our housing crises and cutting back student finance to affordable and appropriate levels.

Mr Gyimah, if you really want to make a name for yourself, there you go.

CHAPTER 5

IN THEIR SHOES

"As our society gets more complex and our people get more complacent, the role of the jester is more vital than ever before. Please stop sitting around. We need you to make a ruckus."

Seth Godin

"Satire is enjoyable compensation for being forced to think."

Edgar Johnson

During the Cameron/ Osborne years there seemed to exude from them that top public school air of surely you realise we were born to lead you so must we really go to the effort of explaining ourselves to you? Of course those in our country that are actually born to lead and certainly don't have to do any explaining are the Royal Family. In both instances I found that from time to time it was fun to put oneself in their shoes and imagine what they are actually thinking and indeed what they would really like to say if they thought they could get away with it.

And then there is that other cast of characters that certainly have no intention at all of accounting for their actions. Naturally

I mean those who sit at the top table of the benighted European Union. To me they lead an Alice in Wonderland existence so why not satirise accordingly?

31 January, 2011

Cameron's open letter to the electorate

If Dave and his Chancellor wrote an open letter to us all, in which they at last came clean on the important issues of 2011, here's what it would say.

Dear Electorate.

My Chancellor and I have decided that we can no longer fob you off with phrases like "we know the path to recovery will be bumpy but growth will soon return". Instead we now acknowledge that honesty is the best policy, so here goes.

We have made much about what a good job we are doing in containing government spending but, in truth, we are barely scratching the surface. The level of our National Debt is six times that which we have disclosed to you as we have taken no account of the actual cost of public-sector pensions and a whole host of other liabilities (see Nick Silver's IEA Bankruptcy Foretold Paper of last June).

This means that the only hope we have of making any meaningful impact on our massive debt is to inflate our way out. I'm sure you will have noticed we have already started down this path, as although inflation is rapidly approaching 6 per cent, we will continue to urge the Bank of England to pay savers just 0.5 per cent for as long as possible. Luckily for us, the so-called bond vigilantes only seem to be able to concentrate on one thing at a time so we are praying that Euroland's Club Med keeps them away from looking too closely at our books for many moons to come. Whatever happens, please accept our apologies because your standard of living and personal wealth is going to fall a long way from here.

This brings us to our policy towards the banks. Our natural inclination is to be chummy with their top people as we rather admire a breed that has as much chutzpah as we politicians. We do realise that Mr Diamond's comments that the time for remorse is over and we now need to be nice to the all important banking community, is not acceptable to you. Actually a spoof "news " item in the current edition of Private Eye sums up reality rather nicely: "A government spokesman insisted that the Square Mile must retain its status as a major player in the meltdown of our economy. If the banks were to withhold bonuses, these City high-fliers would just take their skills for destroying economies elsewhere and surely none of us want that."

You will be pleased to know that we are not going to just bury our heads in the sand as there are a number of positive things we can be getting on with. For example we are going to make sure that our banks deposit and lending operations are ring fenced from their so-called investment-banking activities. If the likes of Mr Diamond wish to continue to try to conjure up profits from thinking up ever more complex financial instruments, then their friends in the Middle East etc can fund that. But we know you, the depositor, has had enough of their "risk management" practices.

Another positive development is that we do understand that we cannot expect you to suffer the burden of rising inflation eating away at your finances as well as inflicting ever higher taxation on you. We are well aware there are a large number of you sitting on cash that you are understandably hesitant to invest in, what could be, a more productive manner. To this end, our next budget will include wide-ranging tax incentives aimed at encouraging the individual to invest in our SME companies. We know that this sector provides our best chance of sustainable growth, yet it has proven the most difficult to finance over the long term (see our recent Green Paper Financing a Private Sector Recovery) especially as our banking friends prefer to hobnob at Davos rather than take a fresh look at Dagenham.

In summary, George and I realise that being honest breaks every political rule in the book but as Greece, Egypt and co are finding out, we live in exceptional times and exceptional measures are called for.

Yours,

Dave.

20 April, 2011

The Queen's AGM statement

"It gives me great pleasure, as your chairman and CEO for nearly 60 years now, to review our progress over the past and present year.

Let me start by congragulating my fellow director, Philip Windsor, on reaching his 90th birthday and showing no signs whatsoever of wishing to retire. Indeed in this age of tedious political correctness it is always so refreshing for the board to know we can rely on Philip to voice his forthright views at all times. Given the Deputy Prime Minister's pronouncements on family connections and the jobs market I am sure we can expect Philip to express his opinion on this topical issue shortly.

The past year has been one of our more successful trading periods. There has been the occasional mishap but nothing like on the scale we have had to endure in so many of our more recent times. Indeed, as I write, awareness of our brand globally has never been higher. I will return to this subject shortly.

Charles Windsor has continued to develop our Duchy Originals business most ably. Together with his senior manager, Camilla, they have unstintingly sought out new markets both at home and overseas, winning many converts to their more natural, easy going style, than was the case a few years ago.

Our one unfortunate trading experience was in the international arena where it was pointed out to our colleague Andrew Windsor that he had been associating with some business contacts of questionable veracity. Unfavourable media comment has undoubtedly damaged our ability to do business in the short term but once Andrew has undergone a period of re-training I am confident that our medium to long-term prospects will not be impaired.

Turning to our investment portfolio the main item of interest has been our stake in the Church of England. Unfortunately its main competitor, the Roman Catholic Church, has been actively trying to lure away some of its best traders. In order to protect our position we are urging the C of E's CEO to adopt a more effective way of addressing the ever more competitive world which his company finds itself in. Meanwhile our property portfolio continues to be of the highest quality though we do expect to have to set aside more financial resources for repairs and renewals as some of the palaces are looking a little tired.

I now turn to what should prove our most exciting news for many years, by which I do of course mean the impending appointment of Kate Middleton to the board. Kate, together with William Windsor, brings a much-needed injection of youth and vigour to the company. Interest in her appointment is expected to make a significant and highly profitable contribution to our business globally for many years to come. An early indication of this is we are in advanced talks with a well-known

Hollywood Animation House to exploit the film star quality of Kate & Wills. Initially it was suggested that a new version of Snow White and The Seven Dwarfs should be made but your board felt this didn't strike quite the right note.

In conclusion, my fellow directors and I are confident that the current year will produce the best trading performance since my great-great-grandmother last led your company and I look forward to reporting this as part of my Diamond Jubilee celebrations in 2012."

Elizabeth Regina

12 August, 2011

Cameron: My post-riot letter to the electorate

Following the last turbulent week, here's what Prime Minister David Cameron would write if he had to update you on the state of Britain today.

Dear Electorate,

Since I last wrote to you earlier this year, so many events have taken place that you deserve an update from me.

Many things have turned out just as I said they would. Inflation is officially expected to top 5 per cent any day now, and Mervyn has told us all that he will hold interest rates to 0.5 per cent so we're well on course to inflate our way out of our dire debt situation. Of course, Mervyn conveniently forgot to tell you that that the markets decide interest rates – not him – as our Mediterranean friends have been finding out.

George is very relieved that the bond vigilantes are still concentrating their ire on our European neighbours. He's also having great fun telling them all that, unlike in WW2, this time we won't be standing in the way of Germany taking over their countries as it really is for their benefit. "Resistance is useless" as someone once said.

Re those naughty bankers, as promised to you last time, we are insisting that if they want to mess around in esoteric financial instruments, we're not going to let your hard-earned deposits finance such goings on. I see Mr Diamond has posed the question "does Britain still want Barclays?" I shall be sending Vince along with the answer, shortly.

I'm sure you will remember in my last letter to you, I did acknowledge that encouraging investment in our SME companies is a sensible way of bringing some growth back into our economy.

I have to admit that we've failed to do much about this – mainly because I can't find any ministers, or indeed anyone left at the Treasury, who is familiar with small companies.

Vince has taken it upon himself to learn about them, but this doesn't come naturally to an ex-chief economist of Shell. Perhaps I should make Sam a minister? After all, she was a director of a small company called Smythson.

Of course, you will all be very worried about the terrible scenes that have been played out on many of our streets recently. Normally I would ask Rupert and Rebekah what to do, but they're having to be punished for breaking all sorts of rules, so we're no longer even allowing them in by way of No 10's tradesmen's entrance.

Really what's needed is a statesmanlike response from me, but sadly I am ill equipped for such. Being brought up by a stockbroker was hardly helpful and my PR work experience equips me to be media savvy – but not much else.

Mind you, boarding at Eton could come in useful, as it's well known that it costs more to keep one of the feral rats (as that shopkeeper lady so aptly described the looters) in jail than it does sending them to public school.

I'm not suggesting we should flood the likes of my alma mater with the dross of our cities, but there may well be a case for bringing back those educational boarding establishments where local councils used to send their more unruly kids 50 years ago.

Tough love is what's needed and Sam is doing her bit by getting me to write out one hundred times each month "I must order schools no longer to come up with daft phrases like 'Darren, are you ready to receive the discipline message?'"

A dominating woman is just so exciting don't you think?!

Yours,

Dave.

24 April, 2012

Alice in our 21st-century Wonderland

With apologies to Lewis Carroll, an adaptation of his classic tale featuring an all-star cast including David Cameron and Angela Merkel.

The cast in order of appearance:

- Alice: The British people
- The White Rabbit: Subprime mortgage bankers
- The Unicorn: Sir Mervyn King
- The Cheshire Cat: David Cameron
- The March Hare: Mario Draghi, president of the European Central Bank
- The Mad Hatter: The Prime Minister of Greece
- The Queen of Hearts: Angela Merkel

One day in 2008, just as Alice was musing on what next to buy for her house, she saw a white rabbit rush past her, wearing a waistcoat and anxiously looking at his BlackBerry. She had never seen anything like that before and, overcome with curiosity, she followed it down a large rabbit hole, never once considering how she would get out again.

Down, down, down she went. Would the fall never come to an end?

After what seemed like an eternity, she arrived in a curious hall with many locked doors. But how to find a way out? After much conflicting advice from a variety of experts who told her to drink this, eat that cake, don't touch that fan, eat this side of a mushroom and not the other, she made her own way into a wonderland of talking mice, racing dodos and hookah-smoking caterpillars. But perhaps the strangest creature of all she came across was the Unicorn, who clearly regarded himself as the financial king of this wonderland.

"Do you know I always thought Unicorns were fabulous monsters. I never saw one alive before," said Alice.

"Well, now we have seen each other," said the Unicorn. "If you believe in me, I'll believe in you."

Alice, fearing for her sanity, eventually came across something reassuringly familiar. A cat. Except this cat was a great big grinning Cheshire Cat, sitting on top of a tree.

"It would be nice if something made sense for a change," said Alice to the Cat. "I don't want to go among mad people."

"Oh you can't help that," said the Cat. "We're all mad here. I'm mad. You're mad."

"How do you know I'm mad?" said Alice.

"You must be," said the Cat, "Or you wouldn't have come here."

Rather than dwelling on this awkward subject for long, the Cheshire Cat directed Alice to the March Hare's house so she could attend a tea party there with the Mad Hatter and his friends.

"Take some more tea," the Mad Hatter said to Alice, very earnestly.

"I've had nothing yet," replied Alice in an offended tone. "So I can't take more."

"You mean you can't take less," said the Hatter. "It's very easy to take more than nothing."

Alice declared it to be the stupidest tea party she had ever been to and quickly journeyed on to the Queen of Hearts' croquet ground in the land of Belgium.

The Queen was impatient for the game to begin. "Get to your places!" shouted the Queen in a voice of thunder, and people began running about in all directions, tumbling up against each other. However, they got settled down in a minute or two and the game began. The players all played at once without waiting turns, quarrelling all the while. Soon, the Queen was in a furious passion, and went stamping about, shouting: "Off with his head!" or "Off with her head!" about once a minute.

Alice began to feel very uneasy. She had not, as yet, had any dispute with the Queen, but she knew it might happen any minute. "And then what would become of me?" she thought. "They are dreadfully fond of beheading people here. The great wonder is that there's any one left alive."

"Sentence first, verdict afterwards," said the Queen.

"But that's impossible," said Alice.

"I daresay you haven't had much practice," said the Queen. "When I was your age, I always practiced for half an hour a day. Why sometimes I believed six impossible things before breakfast. The rule here is jam tomorrow, and jam yesterday – but never jam today."

The Queen had very fixed views on how to govern her disparate subjects although it was obvious to Alice that the

Unicorn and the March Hare had some other ideas. However, her remark to them that "if you drink too much from a bottle marked 'poison', it's almost certain to disagree with you sooner or later" was ignored.

"What a pity," thought Alice.

19 September, 2012

Our best-known "Firm" unwittingly lands a PR Success

The Royal Family, also known as the Firm, has again won publicity with its most valuable asset: the Duchess of Cambridge.

As Terry Wogan used to say, "Is it me?" I wonder whether I'm alone in detecting a large whiff of hypocrisy when it comes to the furore over a topless Kate Middleton?

A while back I mused over what the Queen might write if she had to produce an AGM Statement. After all, the Royal Family is not known as the Firm for nothing. Right back to the days of George V, the House of Windsor realised that if it was to survive in the court of public opinion, it would have to constantly update its image and keep up with the times in which it lives.

To quote from that imagined AGM Statement, "Kate, together with William Windsor, brings a much needed injection of youth and vigour to the company. Interest in her appointment is expected to make a significant and highly profitable contribution to our business globally for many years to come."

You don't need a PhD in psychology to know that the Duchess of Cambridge has rapidly developed into a huge asset for the Firm. Everywhere she goes she is endlessly photographed, and why? Because she is most red-blooded males' idea of a sassy lady and many ladies' idea of the vivacious model they might have been.

In other words she is the Firm's film star. As such, the camera lens will never be far away. She is easily bright enough to have accepted this fact of life when she decided to join.

So, what of the topless photos? Once the initial shock dies down, I expect cool heads at the Firm will realise that they have stumbled into a tremendous win-win situation. In the blink of a shutter lid, every red-blooded male and envious lady all around the world is never going to turn down the chance of clapping eyes on our most glamorous export.

The win is consolidated by what presumably will be many weeks of high profile pursuit around the globe of any miscreants who dare to publish these photos. Currently France, Italy and Ireland are stoking the public's sympathy or curiosity, and that's before things go viral on the worldwide web.

At this stage in the proceedings, my only advice to the Firm is to watch out for any potential pitfalls. One small one came along just this week, when Kate and Wills had to spend the day amongst lots of bare-breasted Solomon Islanders. Even the British press, waiting in trepidation for the results of the Leveson inquiry, couldn't resist pointing out the irony of that one.

11 December, 2012

The Autumn Statement a Tory chancellor should have issued

The Autumn Statement was yet another example of the tinker's tale; fiddle-faddling at the edges, short on vision and long on a sense of weary resignation. Here is what the chancellor should have said to the country:

"Mr Speaker, for too long now we, as a government, have been under the spell of our coalition partners and a slavish fear of upsetting the status quo. Not anymore. For today I am setting before you a radical departure from our ridiculously complicated and stultifying personal tax system. No doubt what I am proposing will encounter severe opposition inside and outside parliament but the time has come for real leadership. The country expects nothing less. Our constituents are fed up with obfuscation and indecision.

Firstly, I am going to abolish income tax banding and national insurance, to replace these disincentives to work and enterprise with a single flat rate income tax of 30 per cent. This will immediately cut the overall tax burden for standard rate tax payers, and act as a major incentive for higher rate tax payers to purchase a greater amount of goods and services. This will stimulate growth and indeed boost tax revenues in so doing.

Secondly, I am going to abolish capital gains tax (CGT). Time and again it has been proven that CGT acts as a major barrier to investment, holds up the passing on of assets to those who can make them work harder, and lowers the overall tax take by preventing the development of companies and their workforces. The only reason we have shied away from this obvious step to date is that we are scared of being labelled as the party of the rich. This is absolute nonsense and real leadership is perfectly capable of withstanding the fallacious arguments of our detractors. It is not a coincidence that some of the most prosperous nations in the world either have no CGT (Hong Kong, Singapore, Switzerland) or have very low rates (USA).

I make no apology for lifting these proposals from the report of the 2020 Tax Commission, published in May this year. I and my predecessors have continuously suffered under the illusion that only our colleagues in the Treasury know best. The time has come to do away with the "not invented here" syndrome.

Of course, it will take time for these groundbreaking changes to our lives to take effect and in so doing galvanise our economy. Thus, in the meantime, we expect a revenue shortfall of between £30 and £40bn a year. In order to address this I intend to halve the defence budget, saving £17bn per annum. We cannot go on with our traditional role of standing beside the USA as we attempt to sort out the trouble spots of the world. Iraq and Afghanistan have exposed the folly of this old style imperialistic policy. We are a small nation, not a superpower.

We will also shortly be holding a referendum as to whether we stay in the EU. We fully expect a "no" vote, thus saving the exchequer a further £10bn per annum in our net contribution to Brussels and many billions more as the accompanying bureaucracy is dismantled. Mr Speaker, I commend this refreshingly dynamic Autumn Statement to the House."

4 February, 2013

Notes from the PM's weekly conversation with our Queen

Ma'am, may I say again what a pleasure and relief it is to be able to confide in you as to what I'm really thinking. If we were Catholics I suppose it would rather be like coming to confessional, only not in such delightful surroundings! Anyway, here goes.

It's been a busy start to the year, what with my speech on Europe, a spot of tax bashing at Davos and a quick trip to Algeria to say sorry for doubting their army's credentials.

I know I shouldn't gloat but I think I've pulled a masterstroke on what to do about Europe. Of course, you and I realise it's about as likely as Prince Andrew travelling on the Tube that Rompuy, Barasso and company will agree to my new terms for our staying in the EU. Splendid, I say! I can go round the country, wearing that pained expression I do so well, proclaiming "I know I said I'd campaign for a yes vote but those beastly stuck in the mud Eurocrats have thrown out all our suggested reforms. So, it is with a heavy heart, that I now urge everyone to vote no." Only problem is that I've first got to get re-elected. Nobody is going to want young panda-chops to run the show, surely?

Do you remember, Ma'am, that a few years ago you asked why no one saw the credit crunch coming? Sadly, high finance is not my forte but I can tell you we will continue to round up all the usual suspects. Actually, I say usual but recently we've found some new ones in the shape of mega-companies that don't feel like paying any corporation tax to your Exchequer. Goes down very well with your subjects, Ma'am, to give these corporations a good public flogging but no chance the likes of Luxembourg and the Caymens are going to buy into my Davos "wake up and smell the coffee" flummery.

Lastly, Ma'am, George asked me to pass on a few words of financial advice. I know he is not an FSA "approved person" but I'm sure you won't mind. He said to tell you that he has agreed with your new Governor of the Bank of England to gradually turn up the inflationary wick, as it were. Easiest way of dealing with our debt problem and very much in the tradition of your illustrious predecessors who faced the same problem. Anyway, George suggests that you might want to get the chaps who manage your assets to switch out of bonds into rather more inflation proof equities. Markets are already getting a little twitchy, what with the ten year bond falling 15 per cent this month and the pound looking a bit rocky.

21 March, 2013

The Diary of George Osborne age 41 ¾

Meet George Osborne, a hapless chancellor writing candidly about taxes, housing, beer and the economy.

Tomorrow is Budget day, which is the most beastly day of the year for me. I have to stand there – for at least an hour – in front of a packed House of Commons with many television cameras and horrible journalists, pretending that I know how to get the economy cranked up again. Crikey.

Anyway, I came up with a whizzo plan, especially as there isn't any money in the kitty to play with. I'm going to pretend that I've listened to all those interest groups that keep bothering me by throwing a little crumb of comfort to each and every one of them. So, I'll take a percent off corporation tax for big companies and if tiddly companies take on another bod, they won't have to pay £2,000 of National Insurance for the pleasure. Note to self: if a couple of thousand quid makes that much difference, then surely the business is in dire straits anyway?

What else? Well, I can keep the floundering pub industry quiet for a while by adjusting the tax on a pint. Then there is the London Stock Exchange – they've been bleating on for years about removing stamp duty from buying shares. I can show how much I like small companies by removing stamp duty from that funny little market called AIM. Another note to self: must ask Mr Rolet why he thinks 0.5 per cent makes such a difference when the market makers operate on at least a five per cent spread between buying and selling shares to me.

I must not forget that we are running out of energy, so I had better give away some tax breaks to the fracking (think that is the right word) industry. I only hope they find somewhere to drill in our little island without bringing the house down.

Talking of houses, here's my biggest idea! I'm going to give just about everyone who wants to buy one a 20 per cent interest free loan and a chance to get a 95 per cent mortgage on a new place to live. Wow, that should really light a fire under our dear old house market! What could possibly go wrong? After all, where I live in London, house prices always go up! So, why shouldn't that be so everywhere else, from Leatherhead to Leith?

Well, that's all the moaning minnies dealt with, but what to do about us having to borrow and print more money? My plan is to tell that new Canadian chappie at the Bank of England to stop sending me – for the umpteenth time – another letter explaining why inflation is more than the two per cent target. Instead, we could get him to assure us that one day we will get back to only a little inflation but just don't quite know when.

I've now been agonising for ages how to capture, in one pithy phrase, the spirit of my Budget. Luckily, David has this clever new Aussie friend called Lynton Crosby and he's come up with "Aspiration Nation". I told Lynton that it felt more like "constipation nation" to me but he said, "Don't worry George, we've got quantitative easing to take care of that."

25 July, 2013

Windsor Holdings Plc. Trading Statement

Your company is pleased to present an update on its trading activities in 2013.

Indications are that we are on course for our most successful trading period ever in our long and distinguished history. A universally high standard of professionalism from our executive team has enabled your Company finally to put behind it the many disappointments of the closing decade of the 20th Century.

Our international brand recognition goes from strength to strength thanks to several significant events. Celebrations marking the 60th anniversary of your Chairman's Coronation have been followed worldwide. In addition, many of our most high profile employees have enjoyed an unprecedented run of sporting success in diverse area such as tennis, rugby and cricket. Even your Chairman was permitted an uncharacteristic broad grin when her horse romped home in this year's Derby. An indication of the importance to us of sporting success is that our Tennis representative, Andrew Murray, has stopped highlighting the Saltire and has taken up our flag of the Union instead.

Succession planning, however, has been at the top of our agenda. This week's arrival of George Alexander Louis has been our most notable achievement in this respect. His birth has attracted an almost unprecedented wave of interest in your Company. His Christian names were carefully chosen. George, for the ability to slay any future dragons. Alexander hinting at greatness, and Louis as a sop to our European neighbours.

Unpaid-for media coverage has been highly favourable from coast to coast and continent to continent. There has been the occasional recidivist publication such as the current Private Eye cover, which consists of three words "Woman has baby" but such is not expected to impact on the general euphoria.

We are experimenting with new ways to monetise our brand recognition and to this end we recently held an event in the palatial surroundings of our Head Office where our Royal Warrant Holders were able to showcase their goods and services to great effect. New avenues for growth are increasingly important, especially as our lucrative Middle Eastern Division continues to find export licences more difficult to obtain due to ever increasing levels of unrest in the region.

There are also indications that our long established joint venture with the Church of England is about to bear fruit. Under its new financially experienced CEO, Justin Welby, it looks set to move into the payday loans market. Its avowed strategy is to prevent the current leading exponent, Wonga, from dominating this lucrative trade. We cannot stop such companies from handling banknotes with your Chairman's head on but we can aim to drive them out of business.

To summarise, we expect to report an excellent set of results for 2013 but we are not resting on our Crown. With a firm line of succession now in place we expect great things from your Company in the years ahead.

Elizabeth Regina.

CHAPTER 6

THE BRUSSELS
DEATH STAR

*"Indeed, if there's one thing a Euro politician despises
and fears more than anything it's the democratic will of
the people. And this is because many of those who run
Europe today were politicised by 60s pseudo-Marxist
utopianism, which they're still determined to impose
on the people – for their own good – regardless of what
the people might want. They believe in centralised
state control: society as a project – their project. It's the
mentality that ran the old Soviet Union, and it's the
mentality that has driven the European Union forward
against the wishes of the European people, imposing a
constitution on the whole of Europe that hardly anyone
was allowed to vote for, and imposing a single currency
on the whole of Europe that's now falling apart at the
seams. But they won't abandon it because they consider
it a vital step on the road to full political union, and the
abolition of all European nation-states under a central
socialist dictatorship."*

Pat Condell

"Too rich to be relevant to the world's poor, [Europe] attracts immigration but cannot encourage imitation. Too passive regarding international security. Too self-satisfied, it acts as if its central political goal is to become the world's most comfortable retirement home. Too set in its ways, it fears multicultural diversity"

Zbigniew Brzeziński

"When it becomes serious, you have to lie."

Jean-Claude Juncker

I suppose I first realised the European Union was in step with the dark side as more and more absurd financial diktats came spewing out from Brussels. The onset of the debt crisis, the ensuing hypocrisy of Germany, the conduct of the Euro elite, the fawning of our establishment, be it the Prime Minister, the Treasury or indeed the financial regulator and the Bank of England, meant Brexit for me.

The City Grumps in this chapter are a cri de Coeur. No doubt some who read these will be staunch Remainers but, to paraphrase the Son of Man, if they help one sinner to repent, I shall be happy Grump.

22 November, 2011

What on earth would Margaret Thatcher think?

David Cameron needs to step away from the glossy magazine pages, go and see Margaret Thatcher, and take a leaf from the Iron Lady's book of leadership.

This winter sees the release of a film about Margaret

Thatcher which, as the Conservative MP Bernard Jenkin observes, "will show Tories what a real, decisive leader looks like". Can Dave step up to the plate?

Not much chance if this week's Sunday Times magazine is anything to go by.

In it you will find 12 pages (plus the cover) of photographs of our PM in all kinds of touchy-feely poses: Dave cooking; Dave at the breakfast table; Dave gazing admiringly at a family fireworks display. You get the picture.

If ever proof was needed that he is happiest living in some sickly cross between a reality TV show and Hello! magazine, then here it is.

Let's hope Margaret Thatcher didn't see this spectacle, otherwise she might want to have ended it all on the spot.

Sadly for her (and the rest of us), she will have seen him fly to Berlin for a sucking up ceremony with the great "Nein" Meister Angela Merkel. Where is the leadership in that?

Thatcher would have squared up to Merkel and said, "Listen dear, from hereon in we will only consider staying in the EU on the following terms: take them or leave them."

Cameron, though, continues to prefer the apparent status of sitting at the top table not realising the legs are coming off.

As Roger Bootle so perfectly puts it in his Telegraph column, our influence "derives not from sitting at the top table but rather from the fact that we are Europe's third largest economy and the eurozone's single largest export market. That influence would not be lost by missing certain intimate dinners. But the political and bureaucratic class, by and large, has no experience of business. They seem to believe that prosperity derives from treaties and agreements. In fact, it emerges from the efforts of millions of ordinary people and thousands of businesses going about their often humdrum tasks – if they are allowed to. Try running a small company under the present employment laws, health and safety regulations and the like, much of it emanating from the supposed fount of our prosperity – Brussels. Do you imagine Chinese businesses labour under such burdens?"

Being the daughter of a grocer, Maragaret Thatcher admittedly had the advantage over an Eton educated son of a stockbroker when it comes to understanding what it takes to build prosperity.

When she came to power, she knew that responsible British citizens had had enough of the endless chaos of strikes and posturing by puffball nobodies.

When is our Prime Minister going to realise that this time around we've had enough of the self same scenes in Europe?

As Bootle went on to say "the only club we need to belong to is the world, of which we are already a member".

Step away Dave from the glossy magazine pages, go and see the "Iron Lady", and take a leaf from her book of leadership.

23 December 2014

The Christmas Story- Brussels Style.

A few days ago I sat down to a Christmas lunch at London's most excellent Bleeding Heart Restaurant with work colleagues and, as is traditional, we kicked off proceedings with a mass cracker pulling. Out popped the usual paper hats and splendidly silly mottos, which as ever is a great way to get all of us into the festive mood.

I particularly liked the joke that fell out of my cracker. Question "Which players can't you trust in an orchestra?" Answer "The fiddlers". Is it too much to hope some of the boys and girls working on LIBOR interest rate swaps floor get that in their crackers this year? Perchance, I then happened to notice what was written on the motto's reverse. It read:

"WARNING. Children under 8 years old can choke or suffocate on uninflated or broken whoopee cushion. Adult supervision required. Keep uninflated whoopee cushion from children. Discard broken whoopee cushion at once. MADE OF NATURAL LATEX RUBBER."

I experienced one of those surreal moments when you think you must have collapsed into a coma and entered a world of disturbing dreams. But no, I looked around at my colleagues and they were all talking away to each other and still making perfect sense (it was early in the lunch!). I read on:

"Bottle opener not dishwasher safe. Please retain this product safety information for future reference".

Well at least I have obeyed the last sentence.

Yes, you've guessed correctly. It comes straight from Brussels' finest. It took me a matter of minutes on Google to unearth the European Union Toy Safety Directive as the source of this Christmas story. You may think whoopee cushions are hard done by but the Directive also proclaims that those whistle blowers, which scroll out into a long coloured paper tongue when sounded, are now unsafe for all children under 14. An EU official, when asked to explain the thought process that went into this Brussels' version of Christmas, admitted the regulation could be difficult to understand but insisted safety experts knew best "You might say that small children have been blowing up balloons for generations but not anymore and they will be safer for it". Our sanity won't.

This evening I shall be at the traditional and wonderful Service of Nine Lessons and Carols in our village church. When it comes to the reading of the Lesson, which describes the three wise men's bestowal of gold frankincense and myrrh to the baby Jesus, I shall offer up a silent prayer to God thanking him Brussels' finest weren't around then to ruin the Christmas Story with their demands that risk warnings be attached to those precious spiritual gifts.

Happy Christmas and an EU free New Year to you.

8 April 2015

The EU referendum debate: Vote for us because we don't trust you

Yesterday the oleaginous Tony Blair ascended the election podium. Standing there in the prosperity of his new, some would say, ill-found wealth, he had the cheek to say what only those who have spent too long in the stifling corridors of power feel is their ordained right. Namely you don't know what is best for you so we'll decide.

Yesterday the spotlight shone on the true mind set of this politician when he proclaimed the British public cannot be trusted to make the "reasonable and sensible" choice in a European referendum.

"Nanny knows best" has been the holy grail followed by all governments and civil servants across the whole of Europe, with the magnificent exception of Thatcher, since anyone of us has been old enough to vote. Ronald Regan's famous line that the nine most terrifying words in the English language is "I'm from the government and I'm here to help" has been forever ignored… until 6 April 2015 that is. Step forward the unlikely hero of the outgoing coalition, Steve Webb.

Tuesday this week will forever be known as Pensions Freedom Day. In an extraordinary act of bravery Webb, the pensions minister, persuaded his coalition colleagues to engage in truly revolutionary thought that nanny doesn't know best and that yes the electorate should be allowed to decide what to do with their pension savings. As sure as the cock crows, this sparked off a cacophony of articles and comment proclaiming such an act to be grossly irresponsible.

A gentleman called Hugh Pemberton, writing in the Financial Times admirably summed up the case against Webb's revolution when he wrote "betting on your ability to manage your savings so you never run out of income is exceptionally risky". Sadly but typically, like our financial regulator who has remorselessly driven our pensions industry deeper into debt instruments, he has forgotten the virtues of making your own equity investments. For history tells the retiree that over the 20 or so years of his life expectancy FTSE 350 companies pay a rising dividend income stream and, unlike a worthless annuity on death, his estate receives the benefit of that equity investment.

Perhaps the new Pensions Wise Guidance Service will see fit to point this out to anyone who feels a little overwhelmed by this unexpected new freedom. Indeed they could do a lot worse than read Andrew McNally's just published book, "Debtonator". McNally advances a compelling argument for long lasting wealth creation through the use of equity as compared to the essentially nihilistic nature of debt. He uses some wonderful illustrations of how debt has got totally out of hand. I particularly liked his point that if you laid all of the world's debt in dollar bills form end to end it would stretch from Earth to Mars and back 50 times!

Thankfully Webb aided by George Osborne, are not alone in turning the tide against "The Blair B*tch Project" as someone described Blair's speech to me yesterday. For example, others in the Treasury and elsewhere have so far been successful in preventing the FCA from strangling at birth the democratisation of investment through crowdfunding. Unceasing vigilance will be required here but the signs are at least promising.

In the USA Senator Rand Paul, the author of "Government Bullies", who is a big proponent of reducing the role of government in people's lives, has just announced his candidature for the Republican nomination for the Presidency.

Despite the efforts of that most unholy of alliances, Blair, Miliband and Sturgeon, the political wind is beginning to blow in favour of giving us the freedom of making more choices in our lives. Fingers crossed 7 May will help that along.

11 May 2015

David Cameron needs to show us what he's made of by "slaying our pesky bogeymen"

After the glorious victory for common sense in last Thursday's general election, various bogeymen have raised their heads. The time has come to slay them.

The first such beastie takes shape in the form of HSBC, which is contemplating whether to move out of London and back to Hong Kong. In 40 years of watching our banks at play, their propensity to make large scale corporate mistakes is always amusing to watch.

If HSBC's board is silly enough to move its domicile to a communist state then it is clearly too silly for our regulators anyway. A recent letter in the Financial Times from Frankie Leung sums up this one perfectly:

"In the pre-1997 colonial days if you asked who governed Hong Kong, the man on the Yaumetei ferry would tell you: the Hong Kong and Shanghai Bank, the Royal Hong Kong Jockey Club and the governor (in that order). In the post-1997 days, if you ask the same question, the answer is: the Chinese Communist Party, the Hong Kong real estate tycoons and the chief executive (in that order). The expatriate Scots should not get nostalgic over the days when the Union flag was flying over the governor's house in Upper Albert Road. Today the five stars is hoisted over the chief executive's residence. Same place, different flag."

Please Messrs Cameron and Osborne, don't waste time concerning yourselves with the likes of HSBC. If this bank really is that headstrong, let it go.

The second bogeyman appears in the guise of our so-called multi-nationals, which, if the media is to be believed, seem determined to campaign against Brexit. Of course they support Europe because their infrastructure is European facing, whereas if they weren't such corpulent lazy entities they would instead be focussing on the real growth markets of the world.

Europe has given them unhealthily easy pickings for too long. Ignore their bleatings on the EU. The time has come to turn their overpaid heads to the bigger picture, which is doing business with the really dynamic economies such as India and the Far East instead of inwardly rotting European has-beens.

The third bogeyman is Scotland. The absurdity of the SNP attracting 1.4m votes and returning 56 MPs to Westminster, whereas UKIP garnered 4m votes in return for one seat, hasn't sunk in yet but it will. By any ordinary standard Scotland is a puny little country and therefore doesn't deserve to be taken seriously.

If this shrill minority is adamant that it is capable of governing itself and in a financially self-supporting manner then we should say "go ahead, make my day". The other 59m of us should waste no more time kowtowing to Caledonia. Of course, if this does happen, I would suggest that any remaining serious businesses up there move south of the border as quickly as they can.

Congratulations Cameron, you have been given a mandate to govern. Show us you really are made of the right stuff by going forth and slaying these pesky bogeymen now.

14 July 2015

Germany Calling: An argument for Britain needing to leave the EU

With a last-minute deal to stop Greece falling out of the single currency almost certain to bring misery, and newspapers alleging that Germany wants to treat Greece as a bust company, The City Grump believes it's high time that the UK left the not-so-unified EU. Last week, in a Telegraph article headed "Germany and Britain must now reshape Europe", the aptly named Wolfgang Novak revealed all. Novak is at the centre of German thinking, being the former chancellor Gerhard Schroeder's senior economic adviser. Much of the article is taken up with the inevitable railing against Greece's financial irresponsibility before slipping comfortably into that old German persecution complex of "why is everyone always picking on us?"

Then out comes the spine-chilling lines: "There is common thinking between Berlin and London. France is too weak to resist – she will join us. It is the hour of Europe it is the hour of Britain".

Deja vu or what? Any student of the run up to the Second World War will recognise this thought process and we all know what happened next. Just in case you might think this is a mere slip of Novak's pen, he warms to his theme with the priceless observation that "what Europe needs is the common sense of Germany, Austria and the Netherlands".

Fortunately for us, although Germany clearly continues to regard itself as the superior European race, it is no longer in the business of conducting military campaigns to prove it.

Accordingly, our best policy must be to steer well clear of Novak's siren calls. In my view this is re-enforced by Germany's stunning hypocrisy on two fronts. Firstly it never tires of slating corrupt Greek society, yet in the Fatherland until 1999 it was not only legal to bribe foreign government officials, but companies could deduct the payments from their taxes. In the case of bribing employees of foreign companies, this tax break extended until 2002.

As Private Eye's "Letter from Berlin" column pointed out: "German taxpayers were subsidising Greek corruption. The tradition still thrives surreptitiously in [Germany's] business culture".

Indeed, those being investigated by the Greek Authorities include Siemans, Daimler Benz, MAN, and Rheinmetall. The letter also reminds us that former Greek defence minister Akis Tsochatzopoulos was convicted in 2013 of accepting bribes from Ferrostaal (submarines), Rheinmetall (anti aircraft system), Daimler Benz (military vehicles) and Krauss-Maffei Wegmann (tanks).

The other breathtakingly piece of hypocrisy is of course Germany's continuing "nein" to country debt write offs. In 1953 more than 20 Western nations (including Greece!) met in London to consider what to do about 16 billion marks of unpaid German debt stemming from the Treaty of Versailles, and a further 16 billion marks lent to Germany after the Second World War by the governments and banks of the US, Britain and France.

Very sensibly it was decided to write off 50 per cent of the total debt and extend the repayment period of the balance to 30 years. This pragmatic solution paved the way to Germany's recovery. Yet again when it comes to Greece and the rest in 2015, Berlin choses "do as we say, not as we do".

The inescapable conclusion arising from the terms of the "deal" with Greece, combined with Germany's attitude to its Eurozone partners, and its hypocritical actions, is Britain should extract itself from the stinking mess that is the European Union. It is neither European nor a Union. It is disparate and irresponsible. Last knockings have been heard. Time to leave.

14 June 2016

The European Union: We are witnessing the end of the empire

Disillusion, deceit, discontent, dishonour, disgrace, mixed with vanity and greed, is the lethal potion that brings all empires down – the oxymoron that is the EU is rotting away. The time has more than come for us to leave and cut our losses, before we are economically and politically drowned in its sea of strife.

It is not surprising the EU is in terminal decline when you realise that 10,000 of its unelected and protected mandarins are paid more than our prime minister. This gilded house of power is presided over by Jean-Claude Juncker, the ex-prime minister of Luxembourg – a country only known for providing tax avoidance on a grand scale. Is it any wonder that such a system produces ineptitude and catastrophe across its 28 satellite states year in, year out?

The 10,000 and their bag carriers have failed the empire's populace in all respects. Euro economies lie in tatters everywhere. Many will never be able to bring their nations' debts down to sustainable levels. Between 20 and 30 per cent of the cream of their youth lie idle. The share of world output accounted for by the 28 current members of the EU has fallen from 30 per cent to 16.5 per cent from 1980 to 2016.

None other than Pope Francis in a recent interview made an interesting observation on some of the inevitable consequences when he said: "They (the media) don't realise that young people don't want to marry, that the falling birthrate in Europe should make us weep, that there is a lack of jobs, there are fathers and mothers taking on two jobs and children are growing up on their own without having their parents around".

Moving from God to mammon, have you noticed that it is a great swathe of those who have founded and built their own successful businesses that are campaigning to leave, whereas those in big business wishing to remain tend to be the journeymen who have stepped into ready-made corporations with ready-made packages? Prominent self-made Brexiteers include Anthony Bamford, John Caudwell, James Dyson, Robert Hiscox, Jeremy Hosking, Tim Martin and Charles Ross. Meanwhile in the "remain camp" lie the salaried bosses of the likes of Airbus, Asda, Astra Zeneca, BAE Systems, BP, BT, Credit Suisse, HSBC, Marks & Spencerand Vodafone.

Politically the Empire has also failed its peoples. The very fact that we are having this referendum is an indicator of that. Even in France, that bastion of European political integration, it is reported this month by the Pew Research Centre that just 38 per cent of their citizens have a favourable view of the EU. The situation is so chaotic that Brussels has already lost the ability to make Hungary and Poland obey its basic political principle of free speech as the media is now under State control in those former communist territories.

Of course EU foreign policy has been inept for years. Back in 1995 when the US brokered "The Dayton Accord," which brought the bloody Bosnian/Serbian/Croatian conflict to an end, the EU was totally ineffectual. Indeed the EU representatives were excluded from almost all the critical negotiating sessions. In its internal history of the deal, the State Department revealed that Holbrooke's team felt "the Europeans had done more to sabotage the talks than help". They were further humiliated by being subjected to full security searches as they moved around the base, while their Americans and Balkan counterparts were allowed to pass unhindered. The head of the French delegation, Jacques Blot, drew the line at sniffer dogs. "For the dignity of France," he reportedly declared, "I will not be sniffed."

Right now we are all having to deal with the total failure of the empire to come up with a considered and effective response to the wishes of millions of political and economic refugees to start their lives again in Europe. In its place has come a unilateral shoddy little agreement stitched together by Angela Merkel and that bastion of free speech, Recep Erdogan. By the way, can anyone name the current EU Foreign Affairs Minister? Or, to give the office it's more empire–like official title, "The High Representative of the Union for Foreign Affairs and Security Policy"? Thought not. It is Federica Mogherini. She is from Italy, since you ask.

And then there is security. This has been thrown into sharp focus, firstly by the empire's so badly misjudged expansionist policy that it has even managed to wake the Russian Bear in the Ukraine, and secondly (horribly cruel irony of ironies) by major terrorist atrocities in the Brussels/Paris heart of the Empire. Weirdly some souls in the Remain Campaign have been putting it about that if we Brexit our security will be impaired. What security would that be? The empire has no army to speak of and if its Intelligence gathering is so good why has France been under a State of Emergency for the last seven months? As ever we will continue to look to NATO and the efforts of our own Intelligences services to keep us as safe as possible. The EU is nothing but a chocolate soldier.

In summary the empire of the EU is now a rotting carcass. If we stay we run the risk of being ever more infected by its demise. The idea that this is a flourishing, dynamic, outward looking entity is so absurd it wouldn't even pass muster as a comedy routine. Instead it is turning in on itself every day. The empire has failed its people.

22 July 2016

ECB drives coach and horses through State Aid Rules. So should we

The European Central Bank (ECB), as part of its stimulus package, has been merrily buying bonds in a multitude of EU domiciled companies at a mind boggling pace of €300m a day. If that isn't mega State Aid then I'm the Dutch president of finance ministers.

Matthew Lynn in an excellent article in 21 July's Daily Telegraph points out that the ECB has been buying corporate bonds in, amongst others, "Glencore, a company which only last year came perilously close to imploding, Telecom Italia, with its massive exposure to the weakest major economy in the world and Lufthansa, a lumbering beast of an airline just waiting to be eaten alive by new and aggressive low-cost carriers".

In other words the EU's foremost financial public authority has been handing out State Aid subsidies to a whole load of grateful enterprises. State Aid is defined as "any advantage granted by public authorities through state resources on a selective basis to any organisations that could potentially distort competition and trade in the European Union (EU)."

I would expect smart Alec ECB lawyers would point out that the close definition is national public authorities and not supra-national authorities but that is mere sophistry. It is 100 per cent clear the ECB is breaking the spirit of the Rule with impunity.

The latest nonsense coming out of Brussels is that in order for VCT and EIS qualifying companies not to infringe State Aid Rules, investment should only take place in less than seven-year-old companies (the limit is raised to ten for those heavily R&D orientated) and cannot be used to assist those companies to make acquisitions. So Lufthansa, Telecom Italia and Glencore absolutely fine but any UK domiciled company outside its infancy, forget it.

On the other hand what's good enough for the ECB should be good enough for Her Majesty's Treasury. It is worth pointing out that some of the statutory legislation implementing this Brussels interference has not reached parliament yet so now is the time for the new chancellor to install some Thatcherite backbone into the Treasury and say "no, no, no".

As Brexit becomes reality we must start to roll back counter-productive EU diktats. Let's start with this destructive VCT/EIS legislation. If you agree then why not get your MP involved? Thank you ECB for showing us the way!

31 October 2016

Taking a look at Europe's many "emperors without clothes" – starting with Mark Carney

One of the great benefits of the outcome of the referendum vote is that it has identified a whole array of emperors who are wearing no clothes. What is the collective noun for such? Perhaps a "bombastic" of emperors. Let's start with the most topical right now, one Mark Carney

My City Grump of 12 July posed the question "Is Mark Carney the most dangerous man in Britain?" Little did I realise then that a whole range of political luminaries from William Hague, Michael Gove, to the Spectator magazine onwards would follow on and demand his head also.

This is hardly surprising though as in August Mark Carney decided to cut interest rates in a knee jerk response to his anti-Brexit stance. For the BoE to have cut interest rates then was verging on the criminally irresponsible. Even the lowliest foreign exchange dealer realises Sterling is a one way bet when Mark Carney cuts and Janet Yellen from the Federal Reserve Bank of New York is going the other way. The result: an increase in the likelihood of stagflation, a buckling banking system that struggles to make a margin and ballooning pensions deficits in funds stuck with liability-driven investment accounting (LDI).

Amazingly most of the traditional financial media, while recognising the whole central banking QE strategy is going off the rails, are horrified that anyone is prepared to attack Mark

Carney in public as it believes this damages that mysterious beast called "confidence". I think markets and most people post 2008 stopped regarding the governor of the BoE as some sort of deity. As Mandy said in Life of Brian: "e's not the Messiah, e's a very naughty boy".

Then we have the emperors who sit in Brussels. They preside over the apparently magnificent and munificent "state" called the single market and woe betide anyone who questions its efficacy. But in reality the single market is riddled with protectionism.

Internally many commercial and financial companies are protected from cross- border takeover as so eloquently reported in none other than the ardently pro EU Economist magazine in May 2014: "As more takeover bids roll out across Europe, France planted its flag on the battlements by publishing a decree on 15 May that extends the government's power to intervene when a firm is at risk of falling into foreign hands. The decree requires would-be foreign buyers to get the blessing of the economy ministry when planning to invest in French firms engaged in energy, transport, water, health or telecoms. A 2005 version put in place limited the government's power of intervention to sectors linked to national defence. 'Economic patriotism' prompted the new decree, said Arnaud Montebourg, France's interventionist industry minister. The communiqué announcing the decree said it was inspired by similar regimes in Europe and elsewhere."

Externally the single market sits behind tariff barriers erected to protect the inefficiency of various members states in the production of many of life's basics such as food and clothing. To put it simply (you can read about this in more detail at http://www.economistsforbrexit.co.uk/a-vote-for-brexit and go to the sub heading " The optimal WTO option and the route to a Free Trade Agreement with the EU") these emperors' clothes maybe protected but they are full of holes.

And what of our political emperors post Brexit? Former prime minister David Cameron, realising he was caught naked, has left the stage altogether. Francois Hollande has the lowest approval rating of any post war French President. German chancellor Angela Merkel's power bases are crumbling and prime minister Matteo Renzi is up against it in Italy. Need I go on?

Of course back here prime minister Theresa May and chancellor Philip Hammond have yet to be really tested. I am not too worried that May will be caught short but I am concerned about Hammond as the signs are he may be falling under the influence of all those treasury officials who have been exposed, along with former chancellor George Osborne, for expecting the UK to grind to halt on 24 June. We shall see.

Talking of the "apocalypse now" contingent, this article would not be complete without a special mention for the Financial Times. This self-styled emperor of the financial press has been so all pervasive in its anti-Brexit stance that it seems to have taken on the role of a kind of Pravda for diehard Remainers. Just to give you a flavour, I'll direct you to a recent editorial, entitled "British Economy sees off Brexit for another day", written by one Lionel Barber who was awarded France's Legion d'Honneur for the FT's "positive role in the European debate".

Mind you, in the same edition one of his senior wingmen, Martin Wolf, may be starting to realise his emperor is beginning to look a bit threadbare, as his article ends with the rather more conciliatory "The British understand that it is possible to be loyal and in opposition. That is where Remainers find themselves. So be it". Which brings me to Jeremy Corbyn… enough said.

15 September 2017

Jean-Claude Juncker: The latest in a long line of European despots

Julius Caesar was an early adopter ("I came, I saw, I conquered"), Napoleon Bonaparte took up the mantle, Benito Mussolini fancied himself as such and Adolf Hitler came within an ace of succeeding. Now we have Jean-Claude Juncker.

Jean-Claude Juncker is proclaiming in his state of the European Union address that the time has come to turn his office of head of the European Commission into that of president of all 27 EU countries.

Here in Britain we don't much care for despots. Indeed in 1649 we cut off the head of the last one, King Charles 1. That heralded the beginnings of our parliamentary democracy and we have been keen to keep it ever since. It is why, quite correctly, the motto of the Brexit campaign was "take back control".

If it wasn't so serious it would be highly amusing to watch the reaction of some of the high profile priests of Remain to Juncker's bid for despotism.

The ageing ex-Shell economist and amateur dancer and now leader of the Liberal Democrats, Vince Cable, spluttered: "He (Juncker) is in the wrong place and he does no favours for the British pro Europeans. He happens to be a very bad choice for that particular job. He represents an extreme federalist position".

George Osborne who has spent nine-tenths of his time pillorying prime minister Theresa May, David Davis et al through his editorship of the Evening Standard seems suddenly to have lost the use of his pen and refuses to comment.

Tony Blair, that ardent advocate of having more referendums until the British people do the right thing and vote Remain, spectacularly misjudged the British mood by holding a well-publicised love-in with Juncker a few days before he made a bid for totality.

Close to home I hope the Irish are taking note of what is going on because under Juncker's vision for Europe they will be returning to serfdom. They will be stripped of their freedom to make their own fiscal decisions, thus destroying the economic power base they have cleverly built by offering the lowest company tax rate in Europe today.

Recently there have been signs that some of the more forward-thinking in Dublin are beginning to understand this (see the Policy Exchange Report written by Ray Bassett, former Irish Ambassador to Canada and very appropriately released on 4July 2017, American Independence Day). I would urge them to join us in breaking free from the tyranny to come.

The battered and bruised Remainers argue that the likes of French president Emmanuel Macron and German chancellor Angela Merkel would never allow Juncker's office to grab the levers of power. The Financial Times likes to quote the Dutch prime minister Mark Rutte's reaction: "Juncker is a romantic. I am more of a, 'when you have visions, go see a doctor kind of guy'."

But the genie is now out of the bottle. Macron and Merkel may muse about constructing a two, or possibly multispeed, EU but Juncker's state of the union speech is brutally logical. He is underlining the inevitable.

If you expect 27 countries to pull together then you have to impose the same rules and standards, fiscal and political, on all of them. I suppose, sadly for him, even his EU compatriots mentally compare Juncker more to the clown Mussolini than the horrendously effective Hitler.

THE CITY GRUMP RIDES OUT

The fact that he can be cast as a figure of fun at this stage does not detract from the probability that mainland Western Europe is yet again one step away from despotism. We are escaping in the nick of time. Ireland, come and join us in doing so.

Brexiteers unite! You have everything to gain from blockchain

In the firmament of Brexit debate emerges an article by Haakon Overli, founding partner of Dawn Venture Capital, published in the Sunday Telegraph. It argues that the use of blockchain can and should be the bedrock for the post-Brexit environment.

Millions of words and thousands of articles have been written about us leaving the EU, yet I regard Overli's article on blockchain as easily the most important so far. Allow me to explain why.

He starts by making an obvious but continuously overlooked point: "We appear to be discussing Brexit in a language that suggests the world hasn't changed since the UK joined the EU in 1973. By thinking more creatively about the role technology could play, we could solve problems that currently seem so intractable."

As an intro to the use of technology Overli says he was surprised by the lack of attention given to David Davis' observation last month that the know-how now exists to create a non-visible border between two countries, citing the example of the US border with Canada in Detroit, where both countries employ a variety of electronic tools such as sensors.

Indeed anyone who uses something as basic as the M25 Dartford Crossing will be very familiar with high speed continuous vehicle identification.

But it is when he turns to uses for blockchain that things really get cooking. To quote: "Negotiators need a crash course in blockchain, the distributed ledger technology that enables multiple parties to share and update records of transactions with no need for a single central authority... blockchain's real selling point is that its mutual ownership can generate trust where it is otherwise completely lacking.

"In fact, blockchain has many potential applications post Brexit- not least as a single central register for tracking all movements across the invisible border Davis envisages."

Crikey! This is looking interesting isn't it? Indeed Overli is just getting into his stride, so we have: "Elsewhere, take customs controls, where the UK is adamant that trade must continue to be free and frictionless even after Brexit. Blockchain is ideally suited to delivering such objectives-the ledger would enable every party involved in a cross-border transaction to access a single book of record in which the goods were recorded, tracked, traced, and charged to the right duties and tariffs.

"Or what about the need for the UK to negotiate and manage a trade treaty covering all goods and services with each of the EU's remaining 27 member states, requiring thousands of new agreements? Here the ability of blockchain to underpin smart contracts could be crucial. The technology even exists for computerised agencies to enter into these smart contracts without human interference."

Do I hear you say very interesting but surely Overli has entered the realms of science fiction here? Absolutely not. Bryan Zhang and colleagues from the Centre for Alternative Finance (CAF) at Cambridge University's Judge Business School, recently released their Global Blockchain Benchmarking Study (supported by Visa and EY). Their findings are very revealing. They were supplied with data from over 200 companies, central banks and public sector organisations.

CAF found that 57 central banks and public sector organisations across 31 countries are involved with blockchain exploration or trials and Europe dominates with 49 per cent of total. And what are government organisations exploring the use of blockchain for? Exactly what Overli is writing about, namely:

- Identity management;
- Ownership records management;
- Business records management;
- Audit trail;
- Document management;
- Government account settlement and reconciliation;
- Logistics; and
- Supply chain management.

The research, carried out in the six months ending May 2017, estimated that more than 500 staff in the public sector (including central banks) are now working full-time on blockchain and many thousands are full-time in the private sector of which the majority are in finance. Here again Overli has a most apposite observation.

"Then there's the all-important financial services sector. Many in the City are terrified Brexit means an end to the passporting system that enables UK-based banks, insurers and investment managers to trade across the EU.

"Leading financial services businesses are already looking at the potential of blockchain to replace stock exchanges and other market places for capital. Such initiatives may in time provide a means for the sector to continue functioning as if Brexit never happened."

Overli's seminal article gives the lie to the Remoaners continual refrain that Brexit is all too difficult to enact and will end badly. That may have been the case if we were still living in 1973 but this is 2017 and Brexit is very much of the moment. As Boris Johnson said a few days ago: "Let's get on with it."

10 January 2018

MiFID II – The mother of all EU turkeys

At a bloated 1.7m paragraphs long, the EU's new MiFID II regulation is a breathtakingly inept response to the international financial crash of 2008.

The founder of the owner of 23 regulated exchanges and market places around the world has called MiFID II, which went live on 3 January, "the worst piece of legislation I have ever seen in the history of my career". Jeffrey Sprecher, the CEO of the Intercontinental Exchange (ICE) is not wrong. It is an absolute stinker.

Markets in Financial Instruments Directive 2 (MiFID II), slow cooked up by Brussels over a mere seven years, is a series of rules which is supposed to create a European-wide legislative framework for regulating the operation of financial markets.

As such, its consequences affect all of our lives as we all employ finance to go about our everyday business. It should then be a thing of clarity, instead it is generating a vast financial fog, which really should come as no surprise the minute you realise that this legislation comprises those 1.7m paragraphs.

If we make the hugely optimistic assumption that the average MiFID II paragraph consists of just ten words then that means it stretches to a total of 17m words. By way of comparison, the King James' Bible makes do with 783,137 words. So the handbook, or if you will, the instruction manual of the Christian world, which has been doing sterling service for hundreds of years, is, at the very least, 21 times shorter.

This is a level of madness worthy of the Mad Hatter's Tea Party. Yet billions of pounds, dollars and euros have been spent by people from Sprecher's organisation onwards in an effort to take it seriously. How Lewis Carroll would have laughed.

No human being or artificial intelligence can possibly digest such a massive turkey. Nor can anyone be expected to come up with a definitive set of compliant actions that will be bullet proof against testing in the law courts. No surprise then that so far just 11 of the EU's 28 members have transposed the MiFID II rules into their national laws.

It should also come as no surprise, as national regulators were propelled towards the cliff edge of this on 3 January, that they decided to blow a sizeable hole in this Brussels turkey. With just hours to go before MiFID II went live, first the German regulator (inevitably), then the British and the French, gave permission to the world's largest future exchanges and clearing houses to take another 30 months to comply.

This fiasco largely leaves the turkey being offered to retail and institutional investors who are supposed to benefit from MiFID II's voluminous attempt to make research reports independent from broking and other services. The reality is that, yet again, the turkey is inedible. James Bartholomew, in his "Diary of a Private Investor" in the 6 January edition of the Daily Telegraph, summed it up with chilling accuracy when discussing his equity investments.

He said: "I investigated most of these companies with the benefit of research from a wide variety of analysts supplied to me by my stockbroker. But earlier this week new regulations imposed by the EU, called MiFID II, came into force. They require brokers and fund managers to pay for research reports instead of getting them in return for putting business their way. My broker has warned me that because of the new rules it will obtain far fewer reports and will probably not be able to let me see them anymore. To put it bluntly, I think this is a violation of personal freedom. It also reduces still further the contact that people should be able to have with the realities of the commercial world. I hope that changes will be made when we exit the EU."

In case you think that is the grumblings of an insignificant private Brexiteer then hear this from Steve Grob, director of group strategy at Fidessa, which supplies trading, investment and financial software to the world's financial community.

He said: "Two things strike me about MiFID II. First is the enormity of the industry effort involved in getting ready and, second, the almost complete insignificance of it all. Does the man in the street feel that today he has been somehow liberated from the clutches of capital markets? Frankly I doubt it."

In a way we should be grateful to MiFID II because it provides the perfect illustration of how absurd the EU has become and why it is essential for us to leave. It is a breathtakingly inept response to the international financial crash of 2008.

Some seven years in the making and all the while assembled by a centralised, largely financially inexperienced army of bureaucrats, accountable to a lightweight parliament in Brussels/Strasbourg made up of second rate national politicians collecting heavyweight salaries and expenses.

Then, having been nodded through by the EU parliament, 1.7m paragraphs of rules are foisted onto overburdened national regulators and their regulated, whipped on by an ever more power grabbing gorgon calling itself the European Securities and Markets Authority.

Truly the mother of all EU turkeys. Truly a Brexit Thanksgiving.

May 14 2018

The millennial "bug" is alive and living in Threadneedle st.

David 'Two Brains' Willetts and his doughty team mates at something with the Orwellian title of The Intergenerational Commission has spent two years coming to blindingly obvious conclusions.

These are that the millennial – defined as being born between 1980 and 2000 – cannot afford to own a house and is weighed down with student debt. I wrote about this in October 2010 (Are baby-boomers inherently selfish?). Perhaps if he'd read that he would have saved time and money.

Anyway, what is enough to make the eyeballs roll is once again we have a bunch of do-gooders chasing off down the classic cul de sac of recommending treatment of the symptoms and not the causes. And what treatment! To quote Sarah O'Connor, a member of the commission: "To help young people with education debts or a deposit for a house, it proposed that the government spend £7bn a year to give everyone £10,000 'citizen's inheritance' with strict limits on its use".

In what might as well be a nod to the recent 200th anniversary of the death of Karl Marx, this forced redistribution is to be largely paid for by a new property tax, with annual rates of 1.7 per cent of the capital value of a home for any properties worth over £600,000 and 0.85 per cent on values below that.

This state of affairs is then rounded off with the usual airy fairy soundbites such as this from commission member Carolyn Fairbairn, who as director general of the CBI, really should do and know better: "The idea that each generation should have a better life than the previous one is central to the pursuit of economic growth. The fact that it has broken down should therefore concern us all."

Enough of this hare-brained pursuit of the symptoms. Let's return to the cause. The Bank of England finally confessed. Until then it had denied that Quantitative Easing (QE) had anything to do with the stratospheric rise in property prices since 2009. I heard it with my own ears at a City dinner when a long-serving member of the MPC (I won't name him to spare his blushes) in answer to my invitation to agree with me that the BoE's QE had let inflation run wild in house prices, would only reply that "we simply aren't building enough houses".

Well now I invite him to eat his words. In a barely-reported BoE research piece, Staff Working Paper Number 720, bank analysts suggested that without QE house prices would be 22 per cent lower by 2014. Voila!

In previous City Grumps I have described governor Mark Carney as the most dangerous man in Britain and indeed millennials, where that Intergenerational Commission found that the number one concern was not being able to own their own home, have every right to regard him as just that, not just "an unreliable boyfriend". The results of the catastrophic asset pricing distortion brought about by QE are everywhere to be seen in housing. Willetts' commission found that the millennial spends on average 25 per cent of their income on housing compared to 17 per cent for baby-boomers.

Chris Watling at Longview Economics records that now mortgage debt accounts for 40-75 per cent of the loan books of most western banking systems, and this is reflected in the result that in the UK, since the advent of the millennial age, mortgage debt has increased eightfold.

Back in symptom-land it is particularly amusing to see Willetts, who as Universities' Minister was the architect of tripling student fees, is suggesting his £10,000 citizen's inheritance bung could be used to reduce students' debt. Whereas the cause of this burgeoning debt burden on millennial and government alike is the lethal cocktail of Tony Blair's decision to propel 50 per cent of school leavers into universities mixed with Willetts' fee tripling.

Contrast this policy to that beacon of economic success, Germany, where only 30 per cent choose to go to university and it is free of charge. I wonder who has struck the better balance. In short the idea of creating a "citizen's inheritance" is the work of establishment types, attempting to cover for those of their brethren who continue to create a deeply unattractive economic and social environment for our offspring. Where are those who have the courage to write reports advocating fundamental changes in financial and political leadership instead of yet more of a sticking plaster society?

June 8 2018

The Maybot: Artificial, yes. Intelligent, no

Being a lifelong Conservative voter I naturally wanted to give prime minister Theresa May the benefit of the doubt. Sadly she has become a figure of derision both at home and abroad. The description of her as naturally robotic, hence "The Maybot", is all too appropriate.

Like dogs, do robots attract one another? In her case it certainly seems so, since she has fallen under the influence of that other cabinet robot, one chancellor Phillip Hammond. The Treasury has been staffed by defeatists for as long as I can remember (since you ask, about 1967) and the prospect of negativity over Brexit has had Hammond and company slavering.

Maxfac? Oh no we can't possibly deliver that in time. Blockchain-enabled export/ import accounting? Don't be silly. Take Barnier and Brussels at face value? Absolutely. Bend over backwards to accommodate the apparent wishes of the political head of a tiny country (the Irish Republic, population 4.7 million) that has some agricultural products wondering back and forth? Naturally. An intelligent leader would by now have realised that the events in the EU have aligned to make Brexit more desirable than ever. But not the Maybot. Since the Referendum:

- The German electorate have told German chancellor Angela Merkel that the EU is broken.
- The French have elected a president that dreams of unattainable French hegemony.
- Southern EU states are in open rebellion against Brussels austerity requirements.
- Northern European states want to put a stop to further Brussels integration.
- Ex Eastern bloc states together with Italy and Austria are determined to put a stop to free movement of migrants.
- Austria and Lunchtime O'Booze Juncker have decided it is time to embrace Russian president Vladimir Putin's gangster regime.
- EU foreign policy remains unclear, ineffectual and a longstanding joke.
- Brussels stupidity is endangering security surveillance as witness the Galileo farce.

Only a fool would not be able to gain the upper hand in Brexit negotiations against this background. Unfortunately in May we have precisely that, an artificial robot with limited intelligence.

So, apart from the Treasury, who amongst the real power in our country remains doggedly determined to defeat Brexit?

Step forward big business. If you spent millions year in ,year out, building up a comprehensive lobby support structure in Brussels, which enabled you to carry on your cosy existence you'd want to defend the status quo wouldn't you?

The Maybot has clearly been programmed by the CBI and company to be terrified of the possible ending of tariff free trading with EU member states. Accordingly, she has become incapable of grasping the fact that EU tariffs average 5 per cent, which is about how much Sterling moves in any six month period. To sacrifice taking back control of our future on the altar of such old fashioned entrenched interests is not acceptable to thinking humans.

A robot, a bureaucracy, or any other artificial construct cannot understand. The Maybot has been given her chance by the Conservative party. She has failed . She must now be ousted. Sajid Javid, accompanied by Messrs Davis, Johnson and Fox, should deliver the message. Will they have the courage to do so? People respect strength, none more so than Brussels. Get on with it.

July 11 2018

Sajid Javid your time is now: Why May's vision for post-Brexit free trade is myopic for business

Prime Minister Theresa May has said we have no choice but to protect our EU-facing trade from destruction other than to go along with continuing to be a rule taker from the Brussels superstructure. This is Grade One nonsense.

For years Patrick Minford's Economists for Free Trade have been explaining why. Their position was written in a seminal paper, entitled 'When we can't agree. Why a world trade deal exit from the EU will be best for the UK'. It will take you 20 minutes to read and digest but here are the highlights.

The first explodes a lie given to us by May that the World Trade Organisation (WTO) is for the birds:

'Some commentators think the WTO is an irrelevant toothless body that will be trampled on by large trading powers like the US. This is false as can be seen by the WTO's judgement on GM foods. Similarly, it has ruled in favour of Boeing against Airbus in a case involving illegal state subsidies.

'The US has a strong interest in upholding the WTO because it can force the EU to open its markets to products that have been scientifically tested, such as GM foods. The EU in turn will want to use the power of the WTO to hold back or complicate as far as possible President Donald Trump's tariff threats.'

The second highlight does away with the Establishment's Project Fear utterance that without the Maybot's Chequers approach there will be chaos at the ports and borders:

'WTO directives about customs procedures – as mandated in the WTO Trade Facilitation Agreement – are uncompromising. Borders must be seamless and state-of-the-art technological practices employed. Developed countries with adequate resources are expected to install state-of-the-art border systems in order that trade should not be impeded.

'These mandated changes were only ratified by WTO members in February 2017. Therefore, many commentators are unaware of their importance. However, as they were initially agreed in November 2013 and built upon existing best practice, most developed counties have been implementing such procedures for quite some time.

'For example, the World Customs Organisation (WCO), an offshoot of the WTO, operates a 'SAFE' Framework of

Standards to Secure and Facilitate Global Trade. Currently, 169 countries are covered by the scheme, including the EU 28. It is based on four principles (Longworth/Bannerman 2018):

1. Requirements for harmonised advance electronic cargo information.
2. Consistent risk management approaches by governments towards security threats.
3. Outbound inspections of high risk cargo and/or transport performed by the exporting nation using non-intrusive detection equipment to avoid holding up goods on arrival.
4. Fast-track Trusted Trader Schemes for businesses that meet supply chain security standards and best practices.

'Following this lead, most countries permit traders to submit customs documentation electronically in advance of the goods arriving at the border. Virtually all submissions of the EU's own Single Administrative Document (SAD), for declaring imports and exports, are made online.

'So, most trade arriving from countries that are members of neither the single market nor the EU Customs Union suffer little or no hold up at the border when entering the EU. There is no reason for this to change after Brexit.'

The third point the paper makes blows away the smoke and mirrors put up by our feeble PM and her associates over Northern Ireland:

'The politics of the Northern Ireland border fanned by party political issues in the Republic together with manipulation of these issues by the EU have put trade across the Northern Ireland border at the centre of Brexit negotiations. These centre on the requirement of there being no 'hard' border requiring the use of border 'infrastructure'. It is important to establish some basic facts:

1. There is already a border: it hasn't gone away. It is a tax, immigration, currency, political, international, excise and security border.
2. This border is not one of Europe's weightier ones. Some 65 per cent of Ulster's trade is internal to the province, 20 per cent goes to the rest of the UK, and 5 per cent goes to the Republic. A miserly 1.6 per cent of the Republic's exports go north, while 1.6 per cent of its imports come from Northern Ireland.
3. To place these traffic flows in context, in an average month 177,000 lorries and 208,000 vans cross the Irish border. In comparison, over a million lorries pass the Swiss-EU border on a monthly basis.
4. The bulk of the trade is highly regular, so it is simple to regulate. There are 13,000 border crossings annually, solely for the production of Guinness. Likewise, movements in the milk trade are predictable, and ideal for ease of monitoring.
5. Ireland conducts one of the lowest levels of physical inspection in the world (1 per cent).

'Given the above, it is not surprising that HMRC has testified on multiple occasions before various select committees that they do not foresee the need for changes in border procedures after Brexit.

'Because of the low volumes of goods and people crossing the Northern Ireland border, implementation of the Maximum Facilitation scheme using electronic customs clearing to avoid any new hardware on the Irish border should be straightforward; as well as wider adoption of trusted trader schemes, derogation for small traders, and a system of self -assessment (which is set out in the EU Customs Code and which is the direction of travel for EU trade with third countries).

'Note that, under the World Trade Deal approach being discussed, there is no need to negotiate a trade deal with the EU.

THE CITY GRUMP RIDES OUT

'Hence, the onerous 'backstop' requirement falls away. Furthermore, freed from the need to negotiate a trade deal with the EU, the UK's need to curry favour with the EU will disappear and the UK will be in a position to challenge the EU to follow their lead in establishing a 'soft' border.

'If the EU were not to establish sensible border procedures thereby unilaterally causing disruption at the border, it would be a breach by the EU of its international commitments as WCO members. These WCO standards are now incorporated into the EU's own Union Customs Code."

Judgement day is obviously here for the Government. The Maybot has been found wanting and incapable of seeing the EU wood from the stout oak trees of free trade. Timid Tory wet Remainers need to read this City Grump carefully and then vote her out. Sajid Javid your time is now. Seize the day.

October 23rd 2018

An Empty Vessel Sinks

It is fascinating to see just how many people looking in on our Prime Minister's Brexit performance are deeply puzzled about her. Is she being fiendishly clever with the EU, so is there something we have missed? Surely she can't be as clumsy and clunky as she comes across to us mere bystanders? Has she mastered the situation?

Sadly the answers to the above three questions are no, yes, and no. Why? Because all becomes clear when we see what is staring us in the face, namely that Mrs May is a born administrator and not a leader. Administrators like to be a given a brief, which they can set about implementing. They invariably think in straight lines. Theirs is not to think laterally, enterprisingly, or think round the subject. Theirs is to deliver what they have been instructed to do. It is plain as a pikestaff that Ollie Robbins and his compatriots at the top of the Whitehall tree realised this when they were asked to turn their minds to Brexit back in 2016/7. Accordingly they duly constructed the now infamous Chequers Proposal and told the PM to get on with it.

Readers of the City Grump will know that for some time now I have dubbed our administrator Prime Minister "The Maybot". As luck would have it a few days ago I was with an old friend who, I discovered, has a number of acquaintances that have worked with her over the years. The frightening thing is that each and every one of them describes the Maybot as an "empty vessel". In other words we have, until now, entrusted someone totally devoid of any leadership ability to take us out of the European Union. Accordingly it should not come as any surprise at all to any of us to see the Maybot, when confronted with the Brussels wall of intransigence, to come up with the limp "can we have some more time please".

This utter farce, more pugnaciously described by ex- Army Tory MP, Johnny Mercer, as a "shit-show", must be ended immediately. Time has run out for our incapable Prime Minister. We must have a born leader as PM, but who? Yes there is Boris but he regularly shoots himself in the foot. Yes there is Michael Gove but he is too Machiavellian for his own good. Yes there is David Davis but he probably doesn't have the stamina/stomach for it.

So who should consign the Maybot to an historical footnote? The answer has to be Sajid Javid. He is bright and business-like. When he arrived at the Home Office he summoned his various administrators and presented them with an Action This Day list. He most definitely won't be in awe of the Brussels and Whitehall machines. He has fought his way up the corporate and political trees. Interestingly Fraser Nelson writing in the October 19 edition of the Telegraph said:

'At a recent Cabinet meeting, Sajid Javid listed the options: if talks fail, he said, there can be an immediate stimulus. A chance to push through long-overdue changes and advertise Britain as a self-confident country, presenting itself anew to the world with tax cuts to show it means business.' Those are the words of a true leader, not a Maybot.

I have heard it said by someone who knew him at Deutsche Bank that he lacks moral fibre. This may well be so as it is not an attribute that is well known among investment bankers, lawyers and other City advisors but like the astute leader he is I am sure he can exhibit moral fibre when he judges it politically correct to do so.

Come on Tory MPs if you want to save yourselves from total humiliation, terminate the administrator and put in a real leader.

November 15 2018

The Brexit "Deal". Quisling stalks our Parliament. An open letter.

Dear Members of Parliament,

The opening sequence of the inestimable film about General George. S.Patton reproduces the speech he gave to the United States 3rd Army. To quote:

"30 years from now when you are sitting round the fireside with your grandson on your knee and he asks you what did you do in the great World War 2? Well, you won't have to say I shovelled shit in Louisiana".

What will you say about how you voted on the Maybot's Brexit "Deal"? Will you say, "well I knew it was giving away our freedom but I acquiesced"?

Isn't it extraordinary that 3 days after we remembered the hundreds of thousands of our citizens that laid down their lives so that we could remain free from subjugation by foreign powers our Prime Minister recommends you check yourselves into Brussels' version of Hotel California?

By the time you read this you will know that we are being trapped into an open ended customs union with the Irish border issue to be decided by the European Court of Justice, and that, to boot, at some indeterminate time in years to come. In other words the Maybot and her advisors propose handing control of our Country to a Foreign Power. These are the actions of traitors. The actions of Quislings in your midst.

You are not born a Quisling. You become one when you decide that your Country can only function when an outside force is in command of your Country. You say to yourself there is no alternative so if I can't beat them then I must join them. BUT in the case of Brexit the alternative is as plain as a beacon of light, and that shines on Canada ++. The Quislings will tell you this ducks the Irish question. They lie. Movement of goods and people is 100% feasible without a physical border. The only thing standing in the way is pygmy political gamesmanship-stamp it out.

Don't look to our Civil Service for succour. Our once great Foreign Office has now fallen so low it even refuses to grant asylum in Britain to the Pakistani Christian, Asia Bibi, facing death threats from fanatics, for fear of provoking violent reprisals against our embassy. Now our foreign policy is being "dictated by the mob" as Tom Tugendhat succinctly observes.

Irrespective of whether you are in the Leave or Remain camp you must vote this treasonous Deal down. If you don't you will be shovelling shit for the rest of your natural.

Yours in hope but not obedience,

The City Grump.

ACKNOWLEDGEMENTS

Thank you to Real Business for giving the City Grump a platform over some 8 years now. Inevitably staff there have come and gone over those years but whoever I have been dealing with at the time has been unfailingly helpful and enthusiastic.

Thank you to Alan Frame and Brian Basham for helping to propel the book forward

Thank you to Mission Control/wife, Karen, and to my children, William and Jennifer for never uttering a discouraging word through the whole process.

Also thank you to all at Matador for holding my hand.